Robert Hendry

RAILS IN THE

ISLE OF WIGHT

A Colour Celebration

No 17 *Seaview* basks in the sunshine at Ryde in May 1964. Built for suburban and branch line duties by the London & South Western Railway in the 1880s and 1890s, the Adams O2 tanks appeared on the Island at the start of the Southern era in 1923, to supplement elderly and run down engines which the Southern Railway inherited from the lines it had taken over. For 40 years, they were the mainstay of services, and have entered railway legend. This was the railway my father took me to see as a small child, which cast its spell over us, and which we photographed together.
Dr R Preston Hendry

Copyright © 1997 Robert Hendry
ISBN 1 85780 053 2

Published by
Midland Publishing Limited
24 The Hollow, Earl Shilton
Leicester, LE9 7NA
England
Tel: 01455 847815 Fax: 01455 841805
E-mail: 106371.573@compuserve.com

Design concept and layout
© Midland Publishing Limited and
Stephen Thompson Associates.

Typeset
in Garamond and
Gill Sans.

Printed in Hong Kong

Front cover, top: **O2 No 14 *Fishbourne* is seen shunting stock at Ryde Pier Head, on a very pleasant but hazy 30th May 1960.**
K L Cook / Rail Archive Stephenson KLC 1129

Front cover, bottom left: **The PS *Sandown* of 1934 approaches Ryde Pier Head in September 1965. She is in Sealink colours with the BR arrow logo on her funnel.** Colour-Rail

Front cover, bottom right: **A Sunday morning at Brading in June 1994, and former London Underground 1938 stock, single set 006, forms the first northbound train of the day.**

Robert Hendry

RAILS IN THE

ISLE OF WIGHT

A Colour Celebration

Midland Publishing
Limited

CONTENTS

Introduction
6

Isle of Wight Railways Map
8

Chapter One
Getting There
9

Chapter Two
Pier, Tunnel and Town
17

Chapter Three
St John's Road
27

Chapter Four
Passenger Stock
35

Chapter Five
The Ventnor Line
40

Chapter Six
Freight and Departmental Stock
56

Chapter Seven
The Central
63

Chapter Eight
Ryde Works
83

Chapter Nine
Despair and Rebirth
85

Photograph on the title page:
The Isle of Wight has attracted countless railway enthusiasts to savour its enchanting railways over the years. Until the 1970s, most chose to photograph these delightful railways in 'monochrome'. A few early photographers used colour, so that scenes such as No 34 *Newport,* pulling away from Ryde St John's Road station in 1952, have survived. The engine is in SR malachite green, but lettered 'British Railways'. The carriages, on this Ventnor line train, are in the carmine livery introduced by the Railway Executive for non-corridor stock. Apart from the rare liveries, the locomotive was one of the first of the O2s to be taken out of service, in August 1955. The photographer who recorded this particular scene was the late S C Townroe. It was in the mid-'fifties that my parents first took me to the Isle of Wight, and as a small child I remember being fascinated by the insistent panting of the engines. I wondered why they were so impatient. They probably were, because the railway was throbbing with activity, but as I grew older, I discovered that the endless panting was the sound of the Westinghouse pump. My father began photographing the railways, and in due course I joined in. This book is the fruit of those visits, with considerable additional material from other photographers and archives. S C Townroe / Colour-Rail BRS 318

DEDICATION

From their inception, more than 130 years ago, down to modern times, the railways of the Isle of Wight have attracted many outstanding railwaymen of all grades. Mark Huish retired to the Island after a brilliant career as manager of the Grand Junction Railway and the London & North Western, and in his retirement, joined the board of the fledgling Isle of Wight Railway. Fifty years later, the Isle of Wight Central Railway was to see a remarkable railway dynasty. Harry Willmott had been manager of the Lancashire, Derbyshire & East Coast Railway throughout its independent life. After it was taken over by the Great Central, he became chairman of the East & West Junction Railway, later re-organised as the Stratford-upon-Avon & Midland Junction Railway. His son, Russell, also moved from the LD&ECR to the S&MJR. Harry Willmott then became chairman of the Isle of Wight Central Railway, and Russell moved to the IWCR offices at Newport, and the combined role of secretary, manager, engineer and locomotive superintendent. Living myself in Rugby, only a few miles from the S&MJR, I became aware of the Willmott connection with the Island when I discovered that Harry Willmott had lived near Rugby. The Willmotts had both known Sir Sam Fay of the GCR, for it was Fay's company which

took over the LD&ECR. Fay, somewhat improbably, became joint receiver and manager of the Freshwater Yarmouth & Newport Railway when that concern ran into difficulties. After Grouping, yet another talented railwayman came to the Isle of Wight when the Southern Railway appointed a

young and resourceful officer to the Island in 1928. Alistair Balmain MacLeod was to become the most legendary of the Island's railwaymen, and was responsible for many innovations such as naming the O2 tanks, the unique Island 'bunker' which gave the engines such charm, and much besides. Retired railwaymen and Island residents still speak warmly of A B MacLeod. By chance I discovered that friends were related to Alistair MacLeod, and it is through the kind offices of Mrs Jean Heritage, that I have been able to include this photo of AB. This book is a tribute not just to Alistair MacLeod himself, but to the railwaymen of all grades who have run these delightful railways over the decades. It is also a tribute to those photographers who recorded the lines so faithfully in colour over the years to enable us to relive or discover for the first time just why those lines are so special and are still held in such affection today. Photograph courtesy of Ewan MacLeod

Below: **O2 No 35 *Freshwater* between Ryde St John's and Smallbrook Junction on the 2.35pm Ryde Pier Head to Cowes service, 4th June 1960.**
K L Cook / Rail Archive Stephenson KLC 1232

INTRODUCTION

The Isle of Wight is England's smallest county. It is shaped like a diamond, with a deep slash at the apex where the estuary of the River *Medina* enters the sea. It is 13 miles in depth, with a width of 23 miles, and has a total area of 147 square miles. The population is just over 120,000, but the Island draws over a million visitors to its shores each year. A chain of resorts run down the east coast, commencing with Ryde, followed by Brading, Bembridge, Sandown, Shanklin and Ventnor. Cowes lies at the apex of the diamond, on both sides of the *Medina*. A chain ferry connects East and West Cowes. Newport, the county town, lies inland where the *Medina* narrows to modest proportions. West Wight is lightly populated with no large communities, Yarmouth, the most important, having a population of about 1,000. The Island, although possessing no mountains, is quite hilly, especially in the south, around Ventnor, and along the coast from Ventnor to Freshwater and Yarmouth. As a result, railway building was costly, and required a surprising number of tunnels for a small Island. Sadly, both Ventnor tunnels, and the Cowes and Newport tunnels are on closed sections, and the only 'active' tunnel is at Ryde Esplanade, where the obstacle was not high ground, but a man-made built-up area. Tourism is important to the Wight economy, but the Island has sophisticated industries, playing a key role in maritime and aerospace work.

Interesting though these 'vital statistics' are, they do not reveal the existence of a transport system of great diversity, with a fascinating history, and which has much to offer the transport enthusiast even today. In the 1990s, the Island is served by state of the art equipment, such as hydrofoils and hovercraft, yet within a few minutes of arriving, one can see a 1930s bus, a 1930s electric train, an 1890s steam locomotive, or a carriage from the 1870s. This is the scene which the current visitor may encounter, yet if one goes back 40 years, there is even more diversity, in which we would include paddle steamers, the first ferries in the British Isles to use Voith-Schneider propulsion, and a fleet of Victorian steam locomotives.

I first visited the Island as a small child with my parents in the early 1950s. The Freshwater, Yarmouth & Newport, Ventnor West, and Bembridge lines had closed, but the Ryde - Ventnor; Ryde - Newport - Cowes; and Isle of Wight Central route from Newport to Sandown survived. Adams O2 tanks dominated the scene, but at Newport, I saw one of the Brighton E1 tanks. On that first visit, my father took a few photos, but they were all black and white. Over the years, we returned to the Island from time to time, and with the exception of a handful of O2s which vanished in the early 'fifties, I saw all the Adams tanks. My father was interested in 'Railways' not just 'Locomotives', so he photographed carriages, wagons and stations at a time when such items were seldom recorded. I cut my teeth on my Grandfather's 12-exposure 120 'Rolleiflex', using black and white film, and one of my first shots of a moving engine was of No 25 *Godshill*, at Cowes. In due course, I was promoted to 35mm and colour film. I had been volunteered to take a few slides when I was about nine, with the camera mounted on the tripod, and told to press the button

'now', but some of the earliest slides composed by myself were of the Adams tanks, and I still recall vividly standing on the footbridge at Newport photographing No 14, *Fishbourne.* It was a difficult slide to take, as I could only just get the engine in the view finder, but it looked dramatic. Happily it turned out fine, and appears in this book.

As late as 1963-64, the stock was well maintained, with locomotives far cleaner than on the mainland, but with closure of the Cowes-Newport-Ryde line and the Shanklin-Ventnor sections, and electrification proposed for what was left, the rot set in. Locomotives were shorn of their nameplates (and if they had not been removed, enterprising 'collectors' would doubtless have done so), lining out was omitted on repaints, and engines and stock deteriorated. It was very sad. Electrification came, using 1923 London Underground stock, which ran until the end of the 1980s, when modern stock, in the shape of 1938 underground equipment, arrived.

The reason that such vehicles have come to the Island, and run long after they have succumbed elsewhere, is found in the restricted loading gauge which precluded most modern stock, unless specially built to the Island loading gauge. Because of its isolation, a sense of pride which still exists in the Island's rail systems, and the use of antiquated second-hand stock, the Island's railways have a unique character, and have long been popular with enthusiasts.

It is not difficult to assess the reasons for the great appeal which the railways of the Isle of Wight possess. They had the charm of the branch line, yet the pace of main line

Ryde shed adjoined the passenger station, and the staff, used to visiting enthusiasts, were obliging and helpful. It was seldom that a 'look round' was denied. A selection of O2 tanks could be seen coaling and watering or going on or off traffic. No 18 *Ningwood,* is on the ash and coal road which ran alongside the shed itself. She arrived on the Island in May 1930, and is seen on 20th May 1964. The O2 tanks were named after Island towns and villages, a brilliant move initiated by A B MacLeod, who ran the lines in the late 1920s and early 1930s for the Southern Railway. Ningwood village was on the Freshwater line, about 3 miles east of Yarmouth. No 18 was withdrawn in December 1965. In the background is No 17 *Seaview,* withdrawn when steam services ended on 1st January 1967.

operation, the quaintness of the Colonel Stephens railways or of the narrow gauge, yet were a part of the mainstream of railways. Like the railways of Ireland or the Isle of Man, they were 'on an Island' yet readily accessible for a day trip, and that trip was normally prefixed by the excitement of a sea voyage. They were big enough to have diversity, yet small enough to know intimately.

Many books have been published on the railways of the IoW, but this is the first full length colour book. With privatisation in hand as this book goes to press, and the changes that will bring, this is an appropriate time for a colour record of some very colourful lines. The earliest image in this book shows an E1 in Maunsell green before the war. More engines appear in malachite green. Coaches are seen in BR carmine, and Southern Region green. Electric sets appear in all-over blue, blue and grey and Network SouthEast colours. There are also dramatic changes in stations, carriages and wagons.

At the time of going to press, Island Line was awaiting privatisation. Unlike the balance of BR, it will be an integrated sale, comprising the entire system, and avoiding the lunacy of separate track, operating, stock and maintenance companies. In this respect the Island is fortunate, as well as unique.

The story behind the book is as involved as the railways it portrays. I first met Tom Ferris and Chris Salter of Midland Publishing in September 1992. They had produced a book on Irish Railways in colour, written by Tom Ferris. Irish Railways have always been a Cinderella subject, and I was impressed. Their faith was justified, as the book sold out. I had known the railways of the Isle of Man from childhood, and suggested a similar colour book. Chris and Tom had faith in that too, and within a month of launch, over a third of the print run had been sold! In conversation with Tom, I mentioned that my father and I had paid many visits to the Isle of Wight, hence this book. We realised that there was amazing diversity. Steam from the 1940s to 1966, the first and second generation Underground stock, and the thriving preserved line, which not only recaptures the O2 era, but has brought back Stroudley 'Terriers' to the Island. The miraculous survival of ancient 4-wheeled coach bodies as hen houses, summer chalets or garden sheds, has enabled the preservationists to recreate traditional IoW trains, using coaches which ran on the Island 70 or more years ago.

Although locomotives or trains form an important part of this book, a railway is much more than its engines, and at a time when few enthusiasts photographed anything but engines, my father turned his camera to good effect on the rolling stock and infrastructure. To offer that record in colour is a particular pleasure, and should be of help to the modeller. Indeed, the needs of the modeller have helped in the selection of a number of views, as I know how frustrating it is to ask what was this like, or what colour should that be?

In the Isle of Man book, although primarily concerned with railways, we looked at the Island's buses, as these were owned by the railway or tramway operators. In the Isle of Wight, the principal bus operator, Southern Vectis, was part-owned by the Southern Railway, (later the British Transport Commission). It seemed logical to include a selection of views of this interesting operator.

Three of the principal ferry routes were railway owned, so we see vessels in Southern Railway, Southern Region, and BR Sealink colours. They help focus the story, and once admitted, it would be illogical to exclude 'Red Funnel' or the independent bus operators, one of whom currently operates the oldest bus on the Island (by a matter of two years).

Unlike the Isle of Man book, where all but a handful of views were taken by my father or myself, I have supplemented our Isle of Wight collection with images from a variety of other sources to round out the coverage, for whilst we covered some aspects in depth, others were not as comprehensive as I would have liked. Nevertheless, my first acknowledgement is to my father, both for encouraging my interest in railways, and for taking the views which form the core of this book. Indeed, some of his shots appear to be unique, for as Roger Silsbury of the IoW Steam Railway says: 'despite an amazing selection of monochrome material, pre-1966 colour is relatively rare'. The rolling stock views in particular are a rarity, and without that added dimension, this book would be much the poorer.

In studying some of the vintage scenes, many of which are unique, we should remember that film speeds were slow and emulsions not always stable, nor did the fully automated camera exist. Today, 200ASA is a normal film speed. Until the 1960s, 25ASA was a fast film. Colour work was difficult other than on a bright day, and dark green coaches and black engines compounded the problem. Given these constraints, the quality of many early scenes is astonishing. Where I have used other photographers' work, the views are individually credited. Photographs taken by my father or myself are not credited individually, for the simple reason that whilst he took the majority of the pre-1970 views, he would sometimes say 'You take this Robert' to give me practice and confidence. Sometimes there would be a helpful suggestion. Often he left me to make up my own mind. In some cases I recall which of us took a specific view, but there are others where I don't know, for with cine, black and white and colour slides, we were both busy everywhere we visited!

Several friends have searched their own archives, including Ron Barry and Richard Martindale, who have contributed scenes which eluded us. Klaus Marx, best known for his long association with the Bluebell Railway, has contributed some absorbing but tragic views of the fate of the O2 tanks. Martin Bloxsom has provided historic items from his collection. In any colour work on railways, there is usually a message of thanks to Ron White of Colour-Rail, whose unique sense of humour added many pleasurable moments to a serious quest. Colour-Rail slides are acknowledged individually, with the photographers name (where known) as well. Thanks also go to George Cammell, BR Shed foreman at Ryde in the early 1960s, to George Wheeler, Andy Snell, Keith Bowden and Jane Aslett of Island Line, and to Terry Hastings and Len Pullinger of the IoW Steam Railway for various facilities. Further photographic contributions have been made by Graham Bell, K L Cook (via Rail Archive Stephenson), Mike Everton, Chris Milner, Peter Robinson and Keith Wheal. A number of views on both systems have been taken from locations not ordinarily open to the public, with the co-operation of the operators concerned, for with modern safety legislation, and in particular the third rail electrification of Island Line, public access is of necessity curtailed when compared to the informality which existed 30 years ago. Roger Silsbury and Richard Newman provided helpful information. Further assistance has been received from Wight-Link, and Michael Archbold and Vicki Thomas for Red Funnel Ferries.

Apart from the railway and transport enthusiast, I hope this book will also appeal to those interested in the Island as a whole, for it shows a fascinating mix of change and timelessness. At Newport and Ventnor, to give but two examples, we see a total transformation; at Ashey, hardly any change. Many books on the Island's railways virtually end in 1966. This is a shame for the electric operation has its own appeal, and serves an important role to this day. Despite a well filled shelf of books on the Island's railways, I was surprised how few covered the first or second generation Underground stock. Jane Aslett, in charge of marketing Island Line, says ruefully that many Islanders seem unaware of their own electric railway's frequent services throughout the day. I hope this book will help redress the balance.

Robert Hendry   Rugby, October 1996

RAILWAYS IN THE
ISLE OF WIGHT

Lines open for traffic as at 1914

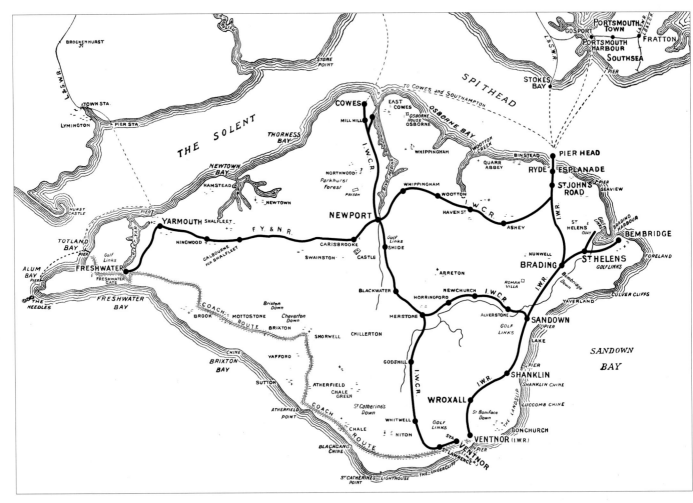

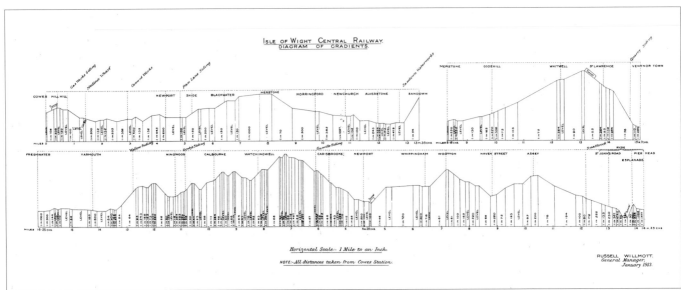

GETTING THERE

Until the 1960s, the majority of enthusiasts who visited the Isle of Wight did so by train and ferry, and no portrait of the Island's railways would be complete without a look at the links which connected Wight with the mainland. There were, and are, a number of routes. The most westerly was between Lymington and Yarmouth, and was associated with the London & South Western Railway. The mainland connection was by means of the Lymington Railway, which was incorporated in 1856 to build a 4 mile route from Brockenhurst, on the L&SWR main line, to the small town of Lymington. The L&SWR obtained powers to lease the branch as early as 1860, but it was not until 1878-79 that matters were finalised. The line was extended from the Town station to a new ferry terminal on the opposite side of the river in 1884. Traffic had been limited in the early days, in part due to the L&SWR concentrating on the Portsmouth services, but with the changes, trains now ran alongside the steamer berth, providing convenient connections. At Yarmouth, passengers transferred to the Freshwater, Yarmouth & Newport line, of which more anon.

The Portsmouth route was much older, sailing packets having operated in the 18th century. The railway involvement began in 1847 when the London, Brighton & South Coast Railway opened from Chichester to Portsmouth. The following year, the section from Cosham became joint with the London & South Western Railway, with the completion of the South Western route from Fareham. As with Lymington, Portsmouth Harbour station was adjacent to the steamer berth. The Lymington and Portsmouth services came into Southern Railway ownership in 1923, became part of British Railways in 1948, and with the privatisation of Sealink, passed to the auspices of the Bermuda based Sea Containers.

A vehicular ferry was instituted between Portsmouth and Fishbourne in 1927, and offers a 24 hour service. A fast catamaran service for foot passengers runs between Portsmouth and Ryde. A Hovercraft service was instituted between Ryde and Southsea in 1965.

The Southampton-Cowes route provided an alternative to the Railway services, and was operated by the Southampton, Isle of Wight & South of England Royal Mail Steam Packet Company Limited. The company adopted the Red Funnel name as being slightly easier to remember! The company operates large roll-on / roll-off ferries running to East Cowes, whilst hydrofoils and catamarans provide a fast service for the foot passenger to West Cowes.

Below: **A selection of SR and L&SWR luggage labels for various destinations on the Island.**

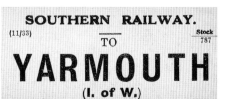

Waterloo - gateway to the South Coast, and the Isle of Wight. I wonder how many holiday makers and railway enthusiasts bound for the Isle of Wight have walked down the platforms at Waterloo, and boarded a train for Portsmouth, Southampton or Brockenhurst. If so, their journey began under the control of this signal box, which was opened by the Southern in 1936. It contained 309 levers, and shortly after it was opened, my father visited it whilst a junior Royal Army Medical Corps officer stationed at Millbank in London. He was invited to sign the visitors' book. Thirty years later, my father and I visited the box together. He told of signing that visitors book many years previously. The book, still in use, was produced, and, there was his signature. He was invited to sign it again.

Above: **For over 30 years following the electrification of the Portsmouth direct line in 1937 the SR's 4-COR stock was associated with services from London to Portsmouth Harbour and the Isle of Wight. A train of this stock headed by 4-GRI unit No 3086 is seen at Portsmouth Harbour in June 1969. The headcode indicates that this particular working was a semi-fast service.** Colour-Rail

Below: **With several vessels damaged or lost on war service between 1939 and 1945, the Southern Railway began to rebuild its fleet as soon as possible, and in a departure from the traditional paddle steamer, ordered a pair of twin-screw motor vessels, the *Southsea* and the *Brading*, in 1946. They entered service in 1948. A third vessel, the *Shanklin* arrived in 1951. All three were built by**

William Denny & Bros Limited of Dumbarton. The *Shanklin* is seen at the stage adjoining Portsmouth Harbour station on 26th July 1972, whilst carrying Sealink colours and the BR double arrow. Originally of 833 gross register tons, the upper deck was extended in the 1960s, increasing her to 986grt.

Right: **The L&SWR took over operation of the Lymington to Yarmouth ferry in June 1884, and it was to remain in railway hands until privatisation a century later. When it is low water at Lymington, it can be difficult to turn a conventional screw driven ship, whilst Yarmouth presents problems in a prevailing south westerly wind. It was for such reasons that paddle steamers survived for so long on excursion and ferry work, due to their greater manoeuverability. Faced with a growth in vehicular traffic, the Southern Railway decided to order a car ferry for the Yarmouth route in 1937, and to fit it with Voith-Schneider propulsion, which consists of a number of feathered horizontal propellers. The TSMV *Lymington* was launched in April 1938, and is seen beside the landing slip at Lymington in 1966. She was built by William Denny & Brothers, and was 132 feet in length, and of 275 gross registered tons. The Voith-Schneider system was then revolutionary, and the *Lymington* pioneered its use in the British Isles. For various reasons, inclined screws were adopted, despite strong protests from Voith's engineers. Their fears were well justified, for she suffered many breakdowns until vertical shafts and horizontal propellers were fitted in 1955, transforming her performance, and prompting an order for a similar ship later on. With the troubles sorted out, she was to serve reliably and efficiently until 1973, when she was sold on for use elsewhere. This was a remarkable tribute to a pioneering vessel.**

Above: **At Lymington Pier, the tracks fanned out just before the platform. An Ivatt class 2 2-6-2T, No 41312, runs round its train on 30th October 1966, prior to taking the 4.27pm working back to Brockenhurst. A level crossing was provided just short of the platform, to provide access for the car ferry ramp.**

Top: **Red Funnel was formed in 1861 out of the merger of the Isle of Wight Royal Mail Steam Packet Co, and the Isle of Wight Steam Packet Co, and over the years was to operate a variety of routes to and around the Island, and to other South Coast resorts. PS** *Princess Elizabeth* **was built in 1927 by Day, Summers & Co, and was the last paddle steamer the company built, shortly before the Northam shipyard closed down. She was 195 feet overall, and was powered by a 2-cylinder compound reciprocating steam engine, giving her a speed of 14 knots. She alternated between Bournemouth and Southampton, and by 1957 was the last paddle-steamer in the Red Funnel fleet. As a small child, I remember seeing her in Southampton Water. In 1959, she was sold to Torbay Steamers Ltd for further use, but**

by the late 'sixties, time was running out for the paddle-steamer throughout the British Isles. In 1967 she was towed up the River *Itchen* to be broken up, but received a last minute reprieve for use in a south coast marina. This fell through, and she was resold for £3,000 to become a floating restaurant on the Thames. After a spell near Tower bridge, she was moved to a permanent berth at Swan Pier, between Cannon Street and London Bridge. Sadly her engines have been removed. We see her at Wapping in March 1971, little altered from her Red Funnel days, and prior to the addition of an aft deck house, and other changes for restaurant purposes.

Above left: *Vecta* was built by Thorneycroft in 1938, and entered service in 1939 a few

months after the SR ferry *Lymington*. She too was fitted with the German-built Voith-Schneider horizontal propellers. It gave her remarkable manoeuverability, and Ron White of Colour-Rail, who provided this slide, recalled her amazing ability to move sideways, or rotate in circles. She was 199 feet in length, and measured 630 gross tons. She suffered damage to her propulsion system during the war, and with spares unavailable due to the hostilities, was laid up for the duration. After the war, she was rebuilt with conventional propellers. As well as operating on the Cowes route, where her car carrying capacity was helpful, she was used on excursions. Colour-Rail.

This page, above right: **The Red Funnel route between Southampton and Cowes has**

always been popular, not least because of the passage down the Solent, with all the activity on Southampton Water. In 1947, Red Funnel acquired a surplus Tank Landing craft, renamed the *Norris Castle*, to cope with vehicular traffic. Four similar purpose-built vessels followed in the 'fifties and 'sixties, one of which is pictured here. At that time, the idea of painting your name on the side of ships had not become wide-spread. Had the Southampton, Isle of Wight & South of England Royal Mail Steam Packet Company Limited wished to place its full title on the 736 ton *Osborne Castle,* the lettering would have been very small, or the boat would have needed lengthening. She was built in 1962 by J I Thorneycroft & Co. of Southampton, and was powered by two Crossley 8-cylinder diesel engines, and was

capable of 14 knots. Seen near the Ocean Terminal at Southampton on 22nd July 1972. She was sold out of service in 1978.

Top: When the company changed its traditional black hull for a more modern livery with red hull, it did put Red Funnel on the side, in capital letters. A new *Norris Castle*, of 922 gross register tons, was built by Thorneycroft in 1968, and was the last of the single end ships derived from the tank landing craft. She was driven by two Crossley 8-cylinder diesels, giving a speed of 14 knots. In 1972, a double ended ferry, the *Netley Castle* arrived, and the two newest 'single enders' were drastically rebuilt and lengthened in 1975-76, reappearing as double enders. *Norris Castle* is seen in May 1989.

Above: Bringing the story right up to date is this superb portrait of *Red Falcon,* on a trial run prior to entering service on 28th October 1994, passing *Red Osprey* in Southampton Water. The house flag, with its triangular white, red, green and blue quarters, symbolises four of the original steamers of 1861, the *Pearl, Ruby, Emerald* and *Sapphire.* The same colours were carried by one of the shortest-lived of the company's ships, the *Gracie Fields* of 1938. 'Gracie' was named after the popular singer, who launched the vessel to a rendition of 'Sing as we Go'. As a memento of the occasion, she received an emerald, ruby, pearl and sapphire brooch, which she came to regard as a lucky talisman. Sadly 'her' ship was not so lucky, being lost during the Dunkirk evacuation in 1940. Red Funnel

Left: In 1923, the SR inherited the L&SWR-LB&SCR joint shipping service on the Portsmouth and Southsea to Ryde routes. It comprised five paddle steamers, four dating from before 1900, some horseboats and a tug. Replacement of this venerable fleet began within a few years. The PS Whippingham was one of a pair of vessels built by Fairfield in 1930. She was 244 feet in length and of 825 grt. With the delivery of these two fast paddle steamers, each licensed to carry 1,050 passengers, capacity on the Portsmouth section was dramatically increased. Prior to their arrival, the maximum number of passengers which could be handled on a summer Saturday stood at 35,000. By the end of the 'thirties, peak arrivals had passed 50,000, with five vessels employed on the Ryde to Portsmouth

service, and two serving Clarence Pier, Southsea. This slide, from 1937, is one of the few known pre-war colour views of an SR paddle steamer. It shows the buff and black funnel, black hull, and pre-war golden yellow bands. Colour-Rail

Top: The PS Sandown of 1934 approaches Ryde Pier Head in September 1965. She had been built by Denny's in 1934, and at 216 feet and 684 grt, was slightly smaller than the 1930 duo. As with most of the Southern Region paddle steamers, she was requisitioned by the Royal Navy for war service as a mine sweeper, a role which she was well suited to, due to her shallow draught and manoeuverability. Until 1964, she carried the traditional Southern buff and black funnel, but for the last few months of her

career, until sold for scrapping in 1966, she bore the new Sealink colours of a blue hull, and red and black funnel, with the BR arrow logo. Colour-Rail

Above: The Ryde of 1937 was the last paddle steamer for the Portsmouth section, and also came from the Denny yard at Dumbarton. As with the Sandown, she was driven by a triple expansion 3-cylinder steam engine, developing 133hp. She was a fast ship, and in favourable conditions, could run between Portsmouth and Ryde in 22 minutes. As with other Southern steamers, she served as a mine sweeper, but shed her war paint during the summer of 1945 to cope with rising demand on the Island services. She is depicted in Southern Region colours near the Clarence Pier, Southsea. Colour-Rail

Top: **In this chapter, we have looked at how passengers used to get to the Island, but we should remember that railway stock had to get there too. This scene is quite remarkable in that it was not taken on the Isle of Wight at all. It shows Nos 35 and 36, in lined BR black, but not yet named, at Southampton Docks in 1949, prior to shipment to the Island. We are lucky that this historic event was recorded on film, and doubly fortunate that it was in colour.** S C Townroe / Colour-Rail BRS 831

Centre left: **After the loco and freight stock deliveries of the late 1940s, almost twenty years were to elapse before more stock needed to get to the IoW. In 1966-67, there was a series of movements as former London Transport 1923 sets were prepared for Island service, and then tested on the South Western main line prior to shipment to the Island. Set 045 heads through Weybridge on trial on 28th March 1967. Colour film showing these trains looking quite incongruous as they pass through Clapham Junction appears on Midland Publishing's video** *Rails in the Isle of Wight: Colour Films 1953-1993.* Colour-Rail

Left: **Another twenty years passed, and more stock for the Island was to be seen on test on the mainland. The as yet un-numbered set 001 leaves Eastleigh on a trial trip to Winchester on 30th June 1989.** Colour-Rail

Chapter Two

PIER, TUNNEL AND TOWN

The section between Ryde Pier Head and St John's Road was a matter of 1¼ miles, yet boasted a pier, a tunnel, several overline bridges and private sidings. The companies who actually built and owned it, the LB&SCR and L&SWR, never ran any trains on it. They built it because the Isle of Wight Railway did not have the money or inclination to do so, and passengers faced a slow and uncomfortable horse tram journey from the Pier head to the IWR terminus at St John's Road. It was joint LB&SCR and L&SWR because the two companies watched one another like hawks where anything involved Portsmouth, as this was a frontier station, jointly worked by the two companies. A new railway pier was built, with steamer berths, and at the landward end of the pier, the line curved round to run parallel with the shore, dropping at 1 in 50 to burrow under Ryde town. The section from St. John's Road to a sea front station at Esplanade was opened on 5th April 1880, and the pier section on 12th July 1880. It was handed over to the IWR to operate. IWCR trains did not run through for some time.

Right: **O2 No 32 _Bonchurch_ is about to run round her train in platform 3 at Ryde Pier Head on 20th August 1963. For the enthusiast used to mainland British Railways, where the vacuum brake predominated, the loud tonk of the Westinghouse pump was the first sign that this was a highly individualistic system, for the Island's railways had standardised on the Westinghouse air brake, and remained true to it to the end of steam. The large cylinder above the side tank is the air reservoir. Another difference was the numeral on the buffer beam instead of a smokebox plate. Bonchurch village, after which No 32 was named, is on the coast between Shanklin and Ventnor. In steam days, Pier Head had two platforms, each flanked by two tracks, giving four platform faces in all. Arrivals were normally in the centre roads, as these were the only tracks with run round facilities, and trains were shunted to the outer platforms during peak periods to free the arrival roads. A scissors cross-over at the station throat completed facilities, for a compact but exceptionally busy little terminus.**

Bottom right: **No 33 _Bembridge_ has shunted a Ventnor train into platform 4 at Pier Head in August 1961. In the background the PS _Ryde_ shows just how convenient rail/ship interchange facilities were. In high summer, tens of thousands of passengers arrived and departed from Ryde every week.**
P J Mullett / Colour Rail BRS 884.

Above: **Car S5 of set 485 043 awaits an early afternoon departure from Pier Head in 1987.** During their career on the Island, the 1923 stock carried three basic liveries, all-over blue, blue and grey, and Network SouthEast colours, although not all stock carried the latter. The Ryde Rail slogan was an amusing pun. By the mid-'eighties a number of the 1923 cars had been taken out of service, and the others were in need of major rewiring. The first car to be dealt with was No 31 in 1984, but the first motor car to be rewired was No 5, which was stopped for overhaul in January 1985. This work was completed in May, but the car did not carry out her trials until 25th July 1985, entering traffic shortly thereafter. Car 5 was one of three vehicles retained after the 1923 stock was replaced in 1989-1990, as a de-icing unit, and for possible use on the Pier shuttle. The 3-car set (Nos 28, 31 and 5) was last used in passenger service in January/February 1991. All three vehicles were withdrawn on 31st

May 1991. As the 3-TIS sets had worked with the 4-VEC sets, rather than independently, it was only in the closing days of 1923 workings that a three 3-car set was used in normal passenger service. They were broken up at Sandown in May 1994.

Above right: **The end of steam services eliminated the need for a run round loop, and the reduction of facilities began before steam services ended, with the southernmost platform, No 1, taken out of use. The southern track on the second pair of platforms, 3 and 4, was also removed. This platform had been narrow for the traffic it handled, and was extended over the disused track bed, with the result that the canopy was only about half the width of the platform. The former platform No 4 was renumbered, becoming new No 1, the old No 2 retaining its number, as it happened.**

Bottom: **Despite electrification, much of the steam age infra-structure still survives, including the signal box and semaphore signals, as 3-TIS set 032 leads a 7-car formation into Pier Head in May 1971.** In the early post electrification era there were as many as five trains an hour at peak periods, but as more and more travellers came by car, frequencies dropped to quarter hourly and then to 20 minute intervals. The drab all-over blue livery looked as lifeless on the Isle of Wight sets as on other BR suburban stock. A new scissors cross-over for the station throat was manufactured at Redbridge in 1975, but never installed, and the old badly worn pointwork and signalbox were later removed, with the Pier being operated as two single tracks, the left hand track carrying the pier shuttle between Esplanade and Pier Head. This service was introduced to cope with boat passengers for Ryde and the bus terminal at Esplanade.
R G Martindale

Top left: **We look from the pedestrian pier, across the tramway pier to the railway pier as set 002 approaches Pier Head station in June 1994. Each set consists of a pair of 1938 cars, one to diagram EA265, the other to diagram 266. Both seat 42 passengers. They weigh 27.5 tons, compared to the 32 tons of a 1923 motor coach seating just 26 passengers. Off peak, services may consist of a single set, but for much of the day, two sets are run in multiple.**

Centre left: **Ryde 'Pier' consists of three parallel piers, the earliest of which was a pedestrian pier which started life in 1813-14. The half mile walk was a deterrent to many visitors, and in 1863-64, a second pier was built adjacent to it, to carry a tramway. Trials with a small steam engine revealed excessive vibration, so the tramway was horse worked. The tramway was extended through the streets to St John's Road in 1871. The rail link between St John's Rd and Pier Head was opened in 1880, and the street tramway abandoned. The Pier section of this tramway survived, and tried gas and later coke-burning steam trams, before reverting to horses, and then in 1886, to electric traction. The Pier Tramway remained independent, and was not taken over by the Southern Railway until 1927, by which time the electric stock was worn out and unreliable. Two Drewry petrol railcars were acquired in 1927, running with some of the older trailers to begin with. Later two more cars came. A pair of cars shuttled up and down each track. Car No 8 is the nearest vehicle in this 1960 portrait of Pier Head.** Harry Luff / Colour-Rail

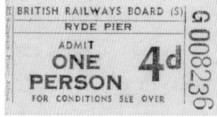

Bottom left: **The Pier cars are popularly remembered for their BR dark green 'EMU' livery, but they were adorned with BR coaching stock carmine, soon after Nationalisation, as in this study at Esplanade.** Colour-Rail

Above: **As Hovertravel's *Double-O-Seven***
basks in the evening sunshine, a 1938 set
rumbles above the waters between Pier Head
and Esplanade. In the background are the
Queen Elizabeth II, the *Canberra*, and the
USS *George Washington*, CVN73, a nuclear
powered fleet carrier. This spectacular line
up of shipping on 4th June 1994 was to
celebrate the 50th anniversary of the D-Day
landings. The *George Washington* is a
'Nimitz' class carrier, displacing over 90,000
tons, with a complement of 6,300 men, half
of whom belong to the air wing, which
deploys over 90 aircraft.

Left: Ryde Esplanade station is built partly
on land, and partly over the water. 485 045
approaches Esplanade in 1987. Although
double track is retained on the pier, the
working for some years has been for
through trains to use the up or landward
platform at Esplanade, outbound trains
reaching the down line via a cross-over
between the station and the tunnel mouth.
The other line was used for the 'Pier Shuttle'
which provided a frequent service between
Esplanade and Pier Head. After delivery in
July 1989, the first of the 1938 sets spent
some weeks on the shuttle, with 1923 sets
on the Shanklin services. By 1990, it was the
other way round, but need for the shuttle
has declined, and a 3-car set of old stock,
retained for shuttle duties in 1991 was never
needed.

Above: **Venturing back more than 20 years, we see No 17 *Seaview* arriving at Esplanade on 21st May 1964. Although carrying the buffer beam disc of a Newport service, the finger board on the platform refers to a Ventnor train, which is how the slide is captioned. Some engines were beginning to show their age by the summer of 1964, and No 17 sports a certain amount of rust around her smokebox. A year earlier such a sight would have been** unthinkable. Seaview is on the coast, midway between Ryde and St Helens. The transition from dry ground to pier is clear in this view.

Below: **There are no trains in sight, so we can study Esplanade station, as it was in May 1964. We see the Barley twist lamps, with their SR enamel target signs, the platform barrows, and even the Pier Tram on the far right.**

Above: **At Esplanade, convenient connections were made with bus services radiating across the Island, the principal operator being Southern Vectis. The company had a complex history, and commenced running buses in 1921 as Dodson & Campbell Ltd. It became Dodson Bros. two years later, but used the 'Vectis' fleetname, which comes from the Roman name for the Isle of Wight. By the late 1920s, it was obvious to the Big Four railway companies that if they did not have some say in road passenger operations, they faced ruinous competition. In 1929, the Southern Railway obtained a substantial stake in Dodsons, changing the name to Southern Vectis, and adopting a green and cream livery. In 1932, the remaining shares in Dodsons were sold to the Tilling/BAT group, which came into public ownership in 1948. When the bus industry was re-organised in the 1960s Southern Vectis became part of the newly formed National Bus Company.**

Tilling group companies had been largely stocked with Bristol buses, as the Bristol works were another part of the Tilling empire. No 608, seen at Esplanade in June 1975, is a Bristol Lodekka FLF6G, of which a number were delivered between 1964 and 1967. The Lodekka concept was developed by Bristol to provide a double decker suited to routes where low bridges existed.

Above right: **Although Southern Vectis achieved a virtual monopoly of stage carriage services within the Island, the route from Ryde along the coast to Seaview had been started by a Mr R Newell in 1922, and under the Seaview Services banner, remained independent. Much of Seaview Services business came from coaching rather than stage carriage services, and in 1992 bus services were disposed of to Southern Vectis, and the company concentrated on coach work. In 1987, the Seaview fleet included** vehicles such as CGA198X, a Van Hool bodied Volvo B58, dating from 1981, and which had been acquired from Harris of West Lothian. This vehicle was subsequently re-registered as PDL230. Van Hool, of Lier near Antwerp, are a leading continental exponent of the high floor luxury coach, and introduced their Alizee range to the UK at the 1980 Motor show.

Below: **Fountain, Crinage & Randall were one independent who entered the Southern Vectis fold, contributing a mixture of Bedford designs from a variety of operators, including Lincolnshire, Maidstone and Shamrock & Rambler. 518 ABL is in the orange and cream Fountain livery, and recalls the classic Duple Super Vega bodystyle of the 1950s, which was developed for the Bedford SB, a type widely used by the British independent coach sector for the best part of twenty years.** R G Martindale

Above: **A beautifully clean No 30 *Shorwell*** pulls away from Esplanade with a Cowes train on 21st May 1964. Over the years, the O2s received a variety of individual alterations. These helped identification. Some engines had prominent rivets on the smokebox hinges; others did not. Some had rivetted fronts to the smokeboxes, some did not. Similar differences existed with buffer beams and smokebox wrappers. As boilers were swapped around, details could change from year to year. Tank patches were another source of variation. Some engines were patched on both sides, others on one side. Many did not need patches. *Shorwell* boasted a riveted wrapper, riveted hinges and patches on both side tanks. Shorwell village is in West Wight, remote from any of the lines, open or closed. The signal to the right of No 30 might appear to be the Esplanade starter, but Esplanade box was closed as far back as July 1922, from when the former platform starter was worked from Pier Head, by lever No 5 in the box there. This upper quadrant signal, with its rail built post, is typical of the many improvements effected by the Southern after 1923.

Below: **Still in steam days, and No 28 *Ashey*** climbs the 1 in 50 grade from Esplanade tunnel into the station, with a Ventnor train on 20th May 1964. This view depicts the extended bunker on the O2 tanks to perfection, the bunker numberplate, and the slotted aperture for the rear coupling. Modellers using sharp curves and prototype couplings, rather than tension lock couplers, sometimes have to resort to such devices, and it is nice to see this 'prototype for everything' shot! With Ashey station on the preserved line between Smallbrook and Wootton, I scarcely need say more about location of the 'name' village! In steam days, the trailing crossover at Esplanade, worked from a ground frame released by Pier Head, was at the seaward end of the platforms.

Left: The location of the train is almost identical to that in the top picture on page 23, but the vantage point differs. 485 041, headed by car S1, and still in blue and grey, pulls away from Esplanade in August 1987. The footbridge, from which this view was taken, was installed to provide convenient public access to and from the Hovercraft terminal. Initially classed as 4-VEC and 3-TIS sets, a cunning adaptation of the traditional Southern electric classification system to create the Island's name, the 1923 stock was later reorganised into 5-car class 485 sets and 2-car class 486, strengthening sets.

Centre left: 485 041 drops down grade towards Esplanade tunnel, after duty on the Pier shuttle. The well used state of the cross-over for through trains is apparent. This set comprised two driving motor cars Nos 1 and 2, a pair of driving trailers Nos 26 ands 27, and a straight trailer No 92. The nearest pair of cars, Nos 2 and 27 were amongst five selected for preservation by London Transport when their career on the Island ended. The fourth vehicle, car No 26, was the first of the 1923 cars to be delivered to the Isle of Wight, on 1st September 1966. It was a part of set 031 until 1985 when it was transferred to set 041. It was condemned on 4th December 1990, and because of its historic interest, was offered to the IoW Steam Railway, but lack of space resulted in the preservation move falling through, and it was later broken up.

Below: By 1994, the 1923 cars were but a memory, and the eastern-most track between Esplanade and Pier Head had fallen into disuse, with the Pier Shuttle no longer running. Trains were being worked on the western-most track, returning to the right line via a cross-over just south of Esplanade station. 002 pulls away from Esplanade as the evening sun streams down at the end of a glorious June day.

Above: **No 22 *Brading* is returning light engine to St John's Road shed, having worked a Ventnor line train into Pier Head on 21st May 1964. Ventnor line trains carried a route disc below the chimney, whilst Cowes/Newport trains carried a disc over the buffers. Six of the O2 tanks, Nos 27 to 32, carried Drummond boilers, with the safety valves mounted on the dome, when they were transferred to the Island before the war. They proved unpopular, due to erratic steaming and priming, and were eventually fitted with Adams boilers. On the mainland, as O2s fell victim to BR standard tanks, a number of low mileage Drummond boilers became spare. Some were transferred to the Island. Latterly there were two such boilers,** which had been on Nos 18 and 27, at the end of the 'fifties, but which were transferred to Nos 22 and 31 in 1963. Once again, they were unpopular, and *Brading* and *Chale* were kept on light duties as much as possible. Predictably the engines differed, the safety valves on 31 being more prominent, due to a lower dome cover, than on 22.

Below: **Thirty years have gone by, and we see 1938 set 003 in the same location in August 1995. The '3' in 003 is blue rather than black, for the formations do occasionally change, and lead car 225 had been transferred from set 005.**

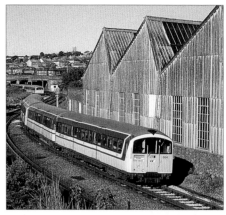

Above: **Thirty years on, in 1994, and instead of an Adams O2, we see Underground set 004. The ground is more overgrown, the signalling has been simplified, but otherwise little has changed. With the Southern Vectis policy of retaining a few veteran Bristol half cab double deckers of the 1950s and 1960s, some of the buses inside the depot also remained unchanged after 30 years.**

Above: **We are able to present two interesting then and now comparisons at St John's. Here No 16 Ventnor approaches Park Road bridge from St John's on 21 May 1964 with a Cowes line train. The tall 'northlight' building to the right is the Southern Vectis garage at Ryde.**

Below: **As my father and I were walking over the footbridge at Ryde St John's station on 20th August 1963, the combination of sunshine and the deep shadows under the bridge appealed to his eye, and this portrait of No 32 Bonchurch, pulling into St John's Road with a Ventnor train, was the result.**

Below: **In 1987 we returned to the same spot to repeat the bottom left scene, this time with 1923 set 485 044. It was fascinating to compare the views we had taken, separated by quarter of a century. Owing to other commitments, we were not able to return to the Island from 1987 to my fathers' death four years later. I am very glad we managed this 'then and now' comparison, as the shot of Bonchurch had always been a particular favourite. Another link between these shots is that as with Bonchurch, the electric stock did not have many years ahead of it when the view was taken. Three of the cars in this set, Nos 7, 44 and 49 were preserved by LT after their withdrawal from Island services. The first set of the replacement 1938 stock, No 001, which arrived in July 1989, was followed by another two sets that year. As a consequence by October 1989, just four sets of old stock remained in use, all down to four vehicles. Another five sets of new stock came in 1990. Two old sets, Nos 043 and 044 were still in use in August 1990, No 044 remaining in service up to 27th September of that year.**

Chapter Three

ST JOHN'S ROAD

On arrival at St John's Road, most enthusiasts made a beeline for the shed. The first shed, which dated from when the IWR opened as far as Shanklin in 1864, was on the east side of the line. In 1874, it was incorporated into the Works and still survives today. Its successor, built in corrugated iron, lasted until 1930, when a new structure, in concrete and asbestos, with a steel frame, was put up. The girders supporting the roof, were second-hand, having started life as overhead line

structures for the LB&SCR's electrification of some of its suburban lines. The LB&SCR high tension 6.7kV AC 'Elevated Electric' system, as it was popularly called, on account of the overhead catenary, was one of two systems inherited by the SR in 1923, the other being the L&SWR DC third rail network. As this was more extensive, the Brighton lines were converted to 3-rail by the Southern in the late 1920s.

It was this new structure which was to become so familiar to enthusiasts.

It adjoined the down platform from which it was separated by two short sidings, which usually housed the breakdown van, stores vans and spare engines.

Below: **On shed at Ryde St John's on 12th September 1959 is No 4 _Wroxall_, one of the two surviving E1 class 0-6-0Ts on the Isle of Wight at this time. This Stroudley design for the LB&SCR had first been introduced in 1874.** K L Cook / Rail Archive Stephenson KLC 800

Above: **A newly repainted No 17 *Seaview*
keeps company with a pair of engines in
malachite green, No 18 *Ningwood*, and the
seldom photographed No 19 *Osborne*, which
went out of service in November 1955. Apart
from the pleasure of seeing such a rare
engine in colour as long ago as 1949, this
view also shows a variant in BR lined black**
livery, with the bunker lining cut off at tank
level, instead of following the contours of
the bunker, and no lining on the splasher.
W Boot / Colour-Rail BRS 126

Below: No 20 *Shanklin*, No 26 *Whitwell*, and
No 29 *Alverstone* feature in this study of the
shed itself on 20th May 1964. Nos 20 and 26
both have patches on their tanks, and
indeed it was the patches which enabled 26
to be identified in this view. In the space
between the tracks, we see the water
hydrants for boiler wash-out.

Opposite page top: No 17 *Seaview* is depicted
at St John's on 4th June 1960. The engine
carries the later standard livery. K L Cook /
Rail Archive Stephenson KLC 1247

Opposite page bottom: Graham Bell's
attractive study of No 14 *Fishbourne* was
taken at the shed on Sunday 3rd October
1965. This angle provides a good look at the
Westinghouse brake pump whose use gave
Wight locomotives their distinctive sound
effects. To the left of *Fishbourne* is
No 31 *Chale*.

Above: **On 20th May 1964, we discover No 33** *Bembridge* **at the top end of No 3 road, along with No 16** *Ventnor*. **Apart from giving an excellent impression of the interior of Ryde shed, these two views show the wheels and chassis more clearly than the usual sun-lit shots.**

Left: **If you wanted to venture inside the shed, it was usually permissible. The engines might be in for boiler wash, or routine attention. Before they went out, they received a thorough cleaning, and to see BR engines kept so spic-and-span well into the 'sixties was a treat. No 29** *Alverstone* **is at the top of the shed on 20th May 1964. Her name village lies a short distance west of Sandown, and was on the Newport Junction line between Sandown and Newport.**

Opposite page, left: **We see the shed in April 1962, whilst a smart school party is touring the depot. On the left No 24 *Calbourne* is sitting on No 2 road, the loco coal and ash road, with a Brighton 5-plank open wagon beyond her. Heaps of locomotive ash around No 24 suggest the wagon is needed to clear away some of the unwelcome by-products of steam power. To the left of *Calbourne* is the incline to the high level No 1 road, serving the coal stage. In the centre is the two road steam shed, and some of the O2 tanks can be glimpsed inside, on 3 and 4 roads.**
No 31 *Chale* is on the right hand road, ahead of the breakdown equipment. She is still carrying an Adams boiler, but will receive a Drummond boiler with dome mounted safety valves in January 1963.

Top: **After the closure of Newport shed in 1958, Ryde had to look after the surviving O2s, of which there were still 19 at the start of the 1960s. The shed building could only hold eight engines, so covered accommo- dation was at a premium. Once engines had been washed out or received repairs, it was important to free the shed to deal with other engines. Whilst we were exploring the shed one day in May 1964, the shed foreman mentioned that they would be shunting the shed in the evening, and moving the engines which had been washed-out on to the coal road incline. This sort of help was typical of the Island railwaymen. We returned on what was a glorious evening, to find No 35 *Freshwater* simmering in the shed yard, ready to perform this shunt.**

Above left: **Four engines were drawn out of the shed, and with her exhaust raising the echoes, No 35 propelled them up the incline out of the way. Reading from right to left, we see No 17 *Seaview*, No 20 *Shanklin*, No 26 *Whitwell*, and No 29 *Alverstone*. A fifth engine, No 36 *Carisbrooke* lies beyond the wagon. Sadly she will never turn a wheel in service again, for she had been stopped with cylinder faults, and withdrawn.**

Above right: **My father felt it was important to record the coal stage and water column, as these are the kind of details which are so often overlooked by photographers.**

Above: **If we look away from the trains, there is much to catch our eye, including elegant IWR spandrels supporting the canopy.**

Left: **St John's Road signalbox, seen in the 1952 view on the title page, came second hand from Waterloo Junction in 1928. In its heyday there were but 7 spares in a 40-lever frame. It survived the modernisation of the system in the 1960s, and other than for more spares, had altered little by 1987. Further changes took place in 1988 with the planned introduction of tokenless block working. This was scheduled for the night of 29/30th October 1988, at which time, Brading and Sandown boxes would be closed, the line singled from Brading to Sandown, with Ryde St John's Road left to control the whole system. Technical problems ensued, and Sandown box was re-instated on 30th October, working tokenless block with St John's, and using the former down line between Brading and Sandown. A new cable was installed, and remote working commenced successfully on 25th February 1989.**

Below: **No 24 *Calbourne* approaches St John's Road with a Ventnor line train on 21st May 1964. The leading vehicle is an ex SE&CR Brake 2nd. From 1926, when Smallbrook Junction signal box was installed, double track working was in force in summer between there and St John's Road. However Smallbrook cabin was taken out of use in winter when the line was not so busy, to save employing an additional signalman there throughout the year. The arms of the signals controlled by the junction cabin were removed and the junction between the Ventnor and Cowes lines was in effect moved to St John's. Single line working on parallel lines was resorted to. In summer, once double track running was instituted, the facing connections at St John's became redundant, and the signal arms controlling them were taken down. Winter working is still in force in this view, as the train is snaking over the cross-over just beyond the platforms. Even if there were no train in the view, the four arms on the gantry would give us the answer. In the background is the breakdown van, DS70008, which had been converted from a Brighton saloon, S6986, in 1959.**

Above right: **As 1923 set 485 044 squeals round the sharp curve, and under St John's Road bridge in 1987, the last vehicle disc is still displayed at the front.**

Right: **It was May 1971 when Richard Martindale caught this line-up of 1923 sets at St John's Road. The nearest car, S7S, is allocated to 3-TIS set 034, but lasted to the end of 1923 stock services, as a part of 5-car set 044. The second car, S23S, was one of the earlier withdrawals.** R G Martindale

Below: **No 21 *Sandown* starts away from the down platform with a Cowes train on 20th August 1963. Extensive wagon repairs are going on in the works yard, whilst No 29 *Alverstone* is on the 25 ton sheerlegs outside the loco shops.**

Above: **No 24 *Calbourne*** drifts along the 'up & down' Newport line (as winter working is still in force) on 20th May 1964. Once double line working has been instituted, and the two lower arms on the bracket removed, the correct description for this view would be that she was on the up main. As I look at this illustration, it brings back happy memories. Within a few days in summer, one could see most of the engines out on the road. There were over 60 timber-bodied passenger carriages in use, and more than 200 wagons, mostly of pre-Grouping origin. Elsewhere the diet was of BR standards, diesels, or DMUs. Pre-Nationalisation coaches were dwindling in number, let alone pre-Grouping stock. The Island was in a wonderful time warp,

and I am glad to have known the railways when a host of O2s fussed back and forth all day.

Below: **'Full House at Ryde'.** A 5-plank open wagon in the loco coal road, engines on each shed road, and breakdown stock on the road to the right of the shed. An up Ventnor to Ryde train, comprising set 490, waits in the northbound platform. Both southbound platforms are occupied, the white discs over the buffers of the left hand train tells us it is for Cowes, the disc below the chimney on the right hand train advises us that it is for Ventnor. The works yard is also well filled, with wagons, Brighton and SE&C carriages and the IWR crane.

Chapter Four

PASSENGER STOCK

Right: S4154, a 6-compartment ex-LB&SCR brake 2nd, has received some sheet metal panelling between two of the passenger compartments in the carriage shops at Ryde St John's on 20th May 1964. As we study the Island passenger vehicles, we will discover extensive sheeting, so it is interesting to see such repairs being tackled. We also see another stop-gap repair, for the louvred door ventilators were complex to replace, and a simple sheet metal hood was substituted where necessary. This could result in different ventilator covers even on a pair of double doors, as in this instance. By the early 1960s, there were ten of these 6-compartment brake seconds in service, S4151 to S4156, and S4163 to S4166.

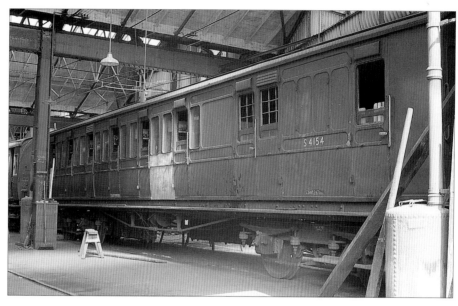

Below left: S4144, photographed in the works yard at Ryde on 21st May 1964, is a 4-compartment ex-SE&CR brake 2nd, ordinarily a part of set 488. Unlike No 4154 which had received only minimal sheeting, much of No 4144's panelling is covered over, suggesting the body is not in good condition. The prominent set number provides an introduction to the way sets were organised in the early 'sixties. By 1962/63 there were 11 diagrammed sets. Seven, 490/1/2/3/4/7/500 were based at Ryde for the Ventnor line. They operated as 3-car sets in winter, with a 4-compartment SE&CR

brake 2nd at the Ryde end, a composite, and a Brighton brake 2nd at the country end. In summer they were made up to six vehicles with spare composites. The four Newport based sets, 485/6/7/8, were used on the Cowes trains, and in winter were similar in formation to the Ryde sets. In summer, they might gain an additional coach, but were not made up to six vehicles, as traffic was not as heavy as on the Ventnor section, and the run round loop at Cowes restricted the length of through workings to Cowes to four coaches in any case.

Below right: S6354, seen at Newport on 9th August 1965, is a Brighton composite. Quoting the length of coaching stock is a vexed subject, for these composites are sometimes referred to as 57ft 7in stock, which is the length over buffers, or 54ft 1in stock, which is the length over the headstocks. The nine survivors in this group (S6348-6356), were intensively used, for being lighter than the SE&CR composites, and with a higher seating capacity, were preferred on the Ventnor services. In summer, it was customary to find one in each of the seven Ryde sets. Klaus Marx

Top left: **S6373 is a 57ft 10in ex-SE&CR composite. As built, it had seven compartments, two with access to lavatories, but with the relatively short runs on the Island, and need for maximum carrying capacity, these had been combined with the adjacent passenger compartments into a large saloon, when sent to the Island. The Chatham composites, of which there were 15, were used in the Newport sets, and as strengthening vehicles on the Ryde sets in summer. No 6373 is seen at St John's Road in May 1964. A similar vehicle, No 6375 survives on the steam railway.**

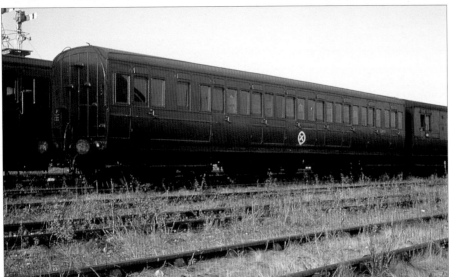

Centre left: **S2451 is a SE&CR 2nd, with eight compartments and a coupe, and is seen awaiting breaking up at Newport in October 1966. In the early 'sixties, there were 69 coaches in use on the Island. As this included 4 full brakes for parcels, luggage, and mails, and as the Ryde-Ventnor sets required 42 carriages, and the Cowes sets a further 16, this only left 7 spares for strengthening and to cover maintenance needs. The stock, though some of the oldest on BR, was intensively used as a consequence.**

Bottom: **The most modern looking bogie stock on the Island, as they showed no trace of wooden panelling, were the four full brakes, S1013 to S1016. In fact, they were of similar age to other stock, and the reason for their flush-sided finish was that they had been converted to full brakes from standard 57ft 10in SE&CR stock. Their primary duties were for newspapers, mail and parcels, but they could also be used for passengers luggage. S1013 was recorded in the carriage sidings at Newport.**

Right: **To the enthusiast accustomed to BR Mk 1s as the staple coaching stock of the preserved railway, the Isle of Wight steam trains are a welcome change, for some of the bogie stock used in steam days was saved from the 1960s. No 6349, a fully panelled Brighton 57ft 7in composite has been restored to Southern green. It was photographed at Haven Street in June 1994.**

Centre: **Second hand coach bodies were keenly sought after in the Island, as an economical way of providing summer houses, farm outbuildings, club rooms or beach chalets. An astonishing number of coaches found their way into such use, and many survive to this day, the heaviest concentrations being around St. Helens and to the west of Cowes. Several have been rescued by the Steam Railway, and using 4-wheel chassis from the ubiquitous SR long wheelbase utility vans, have come back to life. No 4112 was built for the London, Chatham & Dover Railway in 1898, and was transferred to the Island in 1924 to form part of a highly individualistic push-pull set composed of 4-wheelers. This was withdrawn in 1938, but No 4112 survived, and after four years of meticulous work, returned to service in 1991. Even more surprisingly, the other vehicle in the set, No 6369, also survived, and as this illustration reveals, is back in running order.**

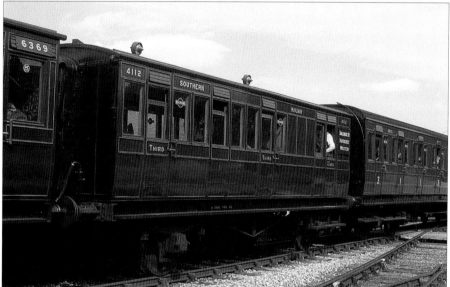

Below: **After No 6369 was completed, work began in the autumn of 1993 on a former LB&SCR Billinton 4-wheel third, No 2343. This dated from 1896, and was sent to the Isle of Wight in 1925, but was withdrawn six years later, and became a bungalow at Gurnard Marsh. Another PMV chassis has been adapted to carry No 2343, and by August 1995, work was well advanced on producing another important vintage coach for the IWR. As soon as this vehicle is completed, it is planned to start work on an LC&DR third, No 2515.**

Above: **With electrification came new types of stock. There were three basic varieties in the 1923 or 'Standard' stock; driving motor brake seconds, driving trailer seconds, and second opens. The 4-VEC sets comprised a pair of driving motor coaches sandwiching a pair of trailers. The 3-TIS sets comprised a driving motor end, a trailer, and a driving trailer. In LT days the latter were known as control trailers, and had a small driving compartment at one end. Car 29, formerly LT 5293, is a driving or control trailer, and is distinguished from the ordinary trailer by the end window and motorman's single door. No 29 is at St John's Road in 1987.**

Centre left: **Car S47, the former LT 7279, is a trailer second open. Unlike No 29 it does not have the end window or driving compart-ment, so it can seat 42 passengers as against 38 on the control trailers. The original 4-VEC and 3-TIS formations later gave way to 5-car and 2-car sets. Latterly all sets had a pair of motor coaches, which, in the 5-car sets sandwiched 2 driving trailers and 1 straight trailer, or 2 trailers and 1 driving trailer.**

Left: **Car 20, the former LT 3308, is a driving motor brake, which by 1987 had been trans-ferred into 2-car set 032. In common with car 22, it differed from the other surviving driving motors in that it was about 18in shorter, although both varieties seated 26 passengers. With the disbanding of set 032 some time later, it became a spare driving motor coach until officially condemned on 12th April 1988. The triangular objects on the roof above the motor compartment are the air vents for the starting grids.**

Above: **Car 7, LT 3209, at St John's Road in 1987.** On some cars, including No 7, the window nearest the sliding doors was plated over, but this was not universal. To cut down on drafts, and provide space for equipment, end doors on the driving motor cars were plated over from the mid-'eighties. Not all cars survived to receive this modification. These changes meant that as with the O2 era, it is doubtful if any two cars, let alone two sets, were identical. Looking from the front of the power cars, whilst the right hand side has a ventilation grill, the left hand side of the equipment compartment is plated over. The reason is that the High Tension contactor cabinets, which should be kept away from any moisture, were on the left hand side of the car body, whilst the compressors and resistances, which needed ventilation, were to the right.

Centre right: **The 1923 stock had been built between 1923 and 1931, and so predated the formation of London Transport itself.** Interior styling was typical of the late 1920s. They had been built for the Northern, Bakerloo and Piccadilly lines. The upswept frames at the driving end were to allow clearance for the motors and the 3ft diameter driving wheels. The unmotored bogies had 2ft 8in diameter wheels.

Bottom right: **1938 set 006 heads north out of Sandown on 3rd June 1994,** and will swing over the cross-over in the distance onto the single track section. The connections on the left, which once led to the Central line from Newport to Sandown, have been retained as a permanent way and civil engineers' siding.

Chapter Five

THE VENTNOR LINE

The Isle of Wight Eastern Section Railway was incorporated on 23rd July 1860 to build an 11¼ mile line from Ryde (St John's Road) to Ventnor, with a short branch at Brading to serve the quay. The Cowes & Newport Railway had been authorised the previous year, and in 1863, the IoW Railway dropped 'Eastern Section' from its title when it obtained powers to build a line to Newport.

The Newport line was to be built, but not by the IWR. The line between St. John's Road and Shanklin was opened on 23rd August 1864, but the formidable terrain south of Shanklin, which embraces the highest ground on the Island, delayed completion of the line into Ventnor until 10th September 1866, the principal difficulty being the three quarters of a mile of tunnelling to reach Ventnor.

The Brading Harbour Improvement & Railway Company was incorporated in 1874 to build a line from Bembridge to join the IWR Brading Quay spur. A sea wall was to be built between Bembridge and St Helens, and the quay at Brading would be replaced by a new harbour at Bembridge. The IWR commenced working the line in 1882, and in 1898, purchased the assets of the Harbour & Railway Company.

Above: **No 21 was built by the Oldbury Carriage & Wagon Company in 1864 for the opening of the Shanklin line. It was donated to the Steam Railway, for restoration.**

Above left: **Cover of the IWR's 1886 guide.**

Above: **This is the only known colour view of an IWR 2-4-0T, and depicts** *Ryde* **in store in the Eastleigh paintshop in 1938, when she had been set aside as part of a Southern museum collection. She is flanked by Beattie 0-6-0 saddle tanks Nos 0334 and 0332.** *Ryde* **was built by Beyer Peacock & Company in 1864 for the IWR, and was un-numbered until Southern days, when she became W13. Operating on the Bembridge branch, she remained in service until 1932. After a spell in store at Ryde, she was moved to Eastleigh, but with the onset of the war she was broken up in 1940 for scrap.** Colour-Rail SR 65

Photographs on the opposite page:

No 27 *Merstone* approaches Smallbrook Junction with a short coal train for Ventnor in 1962. It comprises three ex-LB&SCR 5-plank open wagons, and a standard L&SWR road van. P M Alexander / Colour-Rail BRS 717

No 22 *Brading* takes the Ventnor line at Smallbrook Junction in June 1965. The train has been made up to the usual six coaches, with the first, third and fifth vehicles being Brighton stock, the remainder being ex-SE&CR vehicles. Apart from the different style of panelling, the roof profile is very distinctive. J G Dewing / Colour-Rail BRS 478

Left: **A wealth of detail is encapsulated in this view of No 27 *Merstone*, taken at Smallbrook Junction in 1966. Working the Island boxes, especially the Ventnor line cabins, was demanding, for there was an intensive service on a single track system. The signalman had little time to spare, and had to judge his forays from the box to receive or hand over the staff accurately, for he could not afford to leave the box for long, but being late was even worse. Once he had the staff, he had to remove the token from the leather pouch which was attached to the exchange hoop, and insert it in the instrument. There would soon be a train in the opposite direction, and he would have to offer the train, and then both signalmen would depress the correct keys on their instruments to enable him to withdraw the token. He then had to fit it in the pouch, do up the strap, pull off the signals and hand it to the driver. In a few minutes the whole process would begin again.**
Peter J Robinson

Below: **'A Sylvan setting' is one of the most overworked phrases in the English language, yet it applies to perfection as No 27 *Merstone* heads south past Smallbrook in 1966. The cabin was set amidst the fields and trees, remote from the nearest road, and was an enchanting location.** Peter J Robinson

Above: **Set 001 clatters over the pointwork from double to single track at Smallbrook on 5th June 1994. The junction is worked remotely from Ryde St John's Road. To the left and at a slightly higher level, is the platform for the steam railway.**

Below left: **The 1990s version of Smallbrook Junction is the latest station to open on the Island, and dates from the extension of the steam railway to Smallbrook in 1991. Network South East provided a platform on the Ventnor line. As there is no road, or even pedestrian access, the station is only open when trains are operating on the Haven Street line. Set 006 pulls away from Smallbrook on 5th June 1994.**

Below right: **South of Smallbrook Junction, the line runs through the western edge of Whitefield Wood, providing a tranquil and sylvan backdrop for stock which once burrowed deep beneath London and its teeming multitudes. Set 004 approaches the Harding Shute bridge en route to Ryde on 6th June 1994.**

Top: **No 15 *Cowes* enters Brading in May 1952 with a train of mixed carmine and green stock. She was an early withdrawal, going in May 1956, and was seldom photographed in colour. The Bembridge branch was still open at this time, and the splitting bracket signal from the bay to Ryde or Bembridge is a classic piece of SR signalling.** S C Townroe / Colour-Rail 827

Bottom left: **No 22 *Brading* arrives at her 'name' station, on 6th June 1961, on the 6.25pm Ryde Pier Head to Ventnor service. The branch to Bembridge had closed in 1953 and the track in the bay and the signal controlling it had both gone by this time.** K L Cook / Rail Archive Stephenson KLC 1609

Bottom right: **More than 20 years have elapsed, but whilst the stock has changed, the track layout has altered little. The platform starter has been pulled off as 1923 set 485 044 accelerates away from Brading towards Ryde in the summer of 1987. Instead of the conventional tail-lamp without which no train is complete, the 1923 sets carry a red disc on the rear vehicle.**

Top: There were soon to be substantial changes, for in 1988 Brading and Sandown boxes were closed, the double track section between Brading and Sandown was singled, and the old down platform at Brading taken out of use. It is a Sunday morning in June 1994, and passenger loadings are light for the first northbound train of the day, so a single set, 006, suffices. The swan-necked gas lamps are wonderful survivors from the past, and when the station became unstaffed, they were controlled by a time clock.

Above: Brading signalbox was still in use in 1987, but was to be closed the following year. It was sited on the far side of the Bembridge branch run-round loop, and was so far from the running lines, that a porter was detailed to assist the signalman at peak periods by receiving or handing over the electric train staffs, so that the signalman would not be away from the box too much. The only obvious change since the 1960s was that the Southern Region green and cream paint had been replaced by black and white. The box dated from around 1887, and was fitted with a 30-lever Stevens frame.

Top: **We will take a trip on the Bembridge branch, to see this carmine rake outside the impressive two storey station building in July 1951. Once again the engine is the elusive No 15 *Cowes*. The branch closed on 21st September 1953, although the connections to Brading Quay remained in use until November 1957. Sadly these magnificent buildings have been demolished.** P C Short / Colour-Rail.

Above: **The half-mile long Duver at St Helens provides a popular sandy beach with views overlooking Spithead. Instead of the usual beach huts, a rake of ex Metropolitan Railway coaches, which had seen service on the IWR from the early 1900s, confronts the holiday maker on arrival at the Duver. Until a recent gale, there were no fewer than 11 bodies here, but one was damaged beyond repair, hence the gap in these two rakes of** stock! **As a local enthusiast put it, Medina Borough Council, which owns the stock, had not done any shunting to reform the rake since the gale! This incredible concentration of grounded mid-Victorian coaching stock is unique so far as I am aware.**

Right: **A 4-car train crosses the marshy ground created by the slow moving river *Yar* in the vicinity of Morton Common, just north of Sandown.** For readers familiar with Yarmouth in West Wight, I ought to explain that the Island boasts not one, but two rivers of this name, one predictably emptying into the sea at Yarmouth, the other arising in the high ground between Godshill and Merstone, and running via Horringford and Alverstone, then curving past Brading and reaching the sea at Bembridge. Bembridge Down rises up behind the train. One might question the wisdom of two rivers of the same name in such a small Island, but in the Isle of Man there are three places called Ballabeg, so the Isle of Wight is not unique in this respect. Until local government reorganisation in the 1970s, when it was absorbed into Leicestershire, Rutland, at 152 square miles, was England's smallest county. With recent reforms, Rutland will become a unitary authority, but the Isle of Wight, historically a part of Hampshire so not a contender for the title in the days of yore, has attained County status, and at 147 square miles, wins the 'smallest county' contest by a short head.

Centre right: **The now preserved No 24 *Calbourne* approaches Sandown with the 10.10 Shanklin to Ryde Pier Head working on the 4th April 1960.** K L Cook / Rail Archive Stephenson KLC 1218

Below: **No 26 *Whitwell* powers the 10.10am Ryde Pier Head to Ventnor train near Sandown on the 4th June 1960.** K L Cook / Rail Archive Stephenson KLC 1219

Top: **No 17 arrives at Sandown on the 10.16 coal train from Ryde St John's on 18th September 1962.** K L Cook / Rail Archive Stephenson
KLC 1279

Above: **1923 sets 043 and 044 cross at Sandown in 1987. It is instructive to compare the detail differences between the two cars.**

Left: **The Island's railways had many quaint features, not least some of the signalling. At Sandown, the signalbox was on the platform, not in itself unusual, but the way the 32-lever box was surrounded by and towered above the station canopy, was strange. The signalling equipment was supplied by Saxby & Farmer in 1892, when the IWR caught up with the requirements of the Regulation of Railways Act 1889, and provided for the interlocking of points and signals.**

Top: **From Smallbrook Junction to Brading the line was single track. From there to Sandown there were two tracks. South of Sandown the line reverted to a single track formation. No 30 *Shorwell* leaves Sandown with the 4.25pm Ryde Pier Head to Ventnor service on 20th September 1962.** K L Cook / Rail Archive Stephenson KLC 2496

Above left: **483 002, climbs away from Sandown, past Los Altos and towards Lake bridge, on 6th June 1994. Having been at sea level at Ryde, and not much higher in the marshy area around Morton Common, the line must now climb steeply if it is to tackle the high ground south of Shanklin.**

Above right: **Lake lies between Sandown and Shanklin, the three communities nowadays merging imperceptibly into one another. The Isle of Wight Railway Company opened a station at Lake as long ago as 1889, but it was not a success, and closed prior to the First World War. With residential development in the area, British Rail and the Isle of Wight County Council jointly financed a new station, which opened on 9th July 1987. Set 001 arrives at Lake station on a working from Ryde in June 1994.**

Left: **If Sandown signal box was strange, Shanklin box was bizarre, for instead of rearing up above the canopy, as at Sandown, the windows looked out beneath a specially raised portion of canopy. I can testify from experience that the view was not particularly good! The entrance to the box is via the staircase to the right of the picture. As with Sandown, the box dated from 1892, the equipment coming from Saxby & Farmer. The poster for the Stranraer-Larne steamer service for the *Caledonian Princess* would be a collectors item today.**

Centre left: **In April 1966, services ceased south of Shanklin, which again became the terminus. On 29th October 1966, *Calbourne* has run round her train and shunted it to the up platform. We now have a chance to study this celebrated engine in her last months of BR service. No 24 is in unlined black. Her nameplates have been removed, lest they are pilfered, but replacement plates have been fitted by the railwaymen at Ryde, as they still have too much pride in the job to see their engines shorn of names.**

Bottom left: **The low winter sun, on 29th October 1966, sets off No 24 *Calbourne* to perfection. She has arrived at Shanklin with a train from Ryde Pier Head. Until just a few months previously, she would have waited for a minute or two, and then headed on to Wroxall and Ventnor, but since April 1966, Shanklin has been the southern terminus of the line. The third rail is already in place for the electric services which were to begin the next summer.**

Bottom right: **A 1923 set, 485 044, has drawn up just inches short of the buffer stops which today mark the end of the line. When the IWR opened in August 1864, it was only to Shanklin, and the section to Ventnor was not completed for more than two years. Once again the wheel has turned full circle.**

Above: **In 1979, Southern Vectis acquired six convertible Bristol VRs from Hants & Dorset. Four survived into 1995, although only two were normally used in open top form. No 506 turns out of Atherley Road, Shanklin on the 44 'Big Dipper' route which serves Sandown, Lake and Shanklin.**

Centre right: **One of the most extra-ordinary vehicles in the Southern Vectis fleet is No 864, TDL564K, otherwise known as Shanklin's Pony! This 1971 Bristol RELL was converted to open top in June 1986, for the 44 route. She is on the Esplanade at Shanklin in August 1995. To the right is an A34 'Comet' tank, a design introduced in 1944, and which saw service in the closing months of the Second World War. She is part of a D-day/VE-day exhibition at Shanklin.**

Right: **Shanklin Old Village lies south of the modern resort, and is an enchanting location with thatched cottages and palm trees, through which the main road snakes. It was the late Bill Lambden, a distinguished bus and coach journalist, and later manager of the Isle of Man Railway and Road Services, who first gave me a photograph of Shanklin Old Village. I have included this portrait of Leyland Olympian 743, one of nine buses acquired in 1993 for the Island Explorer service, routes 7/7A, as a tribute to a great transport man, and to show this delightful location. 743 was the last Olympian ordered by Southern Vectis prior to the take-over by Volvo of the Leyland works, and renaming of the type as the Volvo Olympian.**

Opposite page, top: **No 18 *Ningwood* arrives at Wroxall on 3rd June 1960 with the 5.25pm train from Ventnor to Ryde St. John's.** K L Cook / Rail Archive Stephenson KLC 1214

Opposite page, bottom: **South of Shanklin, the line swung sharply inland to skirt the hilly terrain around Shanklin Down and Wroxall Down. The next station, Wroxall, served a small village, nestling just to the north of the high ground. It was a delightful little station with a road bridge at one end and an ornamental cast iron footbridge at the south end. We are looking north towards Ryde on 21st August 1963. The station was signalled from a 12-lever ground frame housed in the ticket office on the up platform. An industrial estate now occupies the station site.**

This page top: **As steam and smoke billow out of the tunnel at Ventnor, No 18 *Ningwood*, shunts in June 1964. The concrete supports for the running in board and concrete hut partially hidden by No 18 are evidence of Southern improvements to the system. The signalbox dated from 1877, and housed a 15-lever frame.** J P Mullett / Colour-Rail BRS 314

Right: **No 35 *Freshwater* has arrived with the 3.25pm from Pier Head on 2nd June 1963. This study from the buffer stops shows the run-round loop, island platform, water column and telephone kiosk.** Klaus Marx

Opposite page, top: **No 26 *Whitwell* arrives at Ventnor with the 10.25am train from Ryde Pier Head on 31st May 1960.** K L Cook / Rail Archive Stephenson KLC 1147

Opposite page, bottom: **As No 26 runs round her train, these views show the cramped site of the station to good effect.** K L Cook / Rail Archive Stephenson KLC 1148

This page, right: **A young fireman removes ash from the smokebox of No 33 *Bembridge* at Ventnor, in May 1965.** Keith Wheal

Bottom left: **The signalman has pulled off, allowing No 27 *Merstone* to head into the stygian darkness of Ventnor tunnel. The station was most peculiar for the platform from which this view was taken, was flanked by tracks on both sides, with a run-round at the south end. No footbridge was ever provided, and access to this platform was either through a train in the right hand road, or by means of 'ship's gangways', one of which is visible in the right foreground. Had an enthusiast invented such a station, with a tunnel at the station throat complicating all shunting moves, and a platform inaccessible other than by a movable gangway, he would have courted derision. However it really did exist!**

Bottom right: **The station site is now an industrial estate, and few traces of the railway remain. There is an old gate, a few fence posts, and most notably the tunnel. It is fenced off and gated today, but still serves a useful function, as Southern Water utilise it for their water main, whilst additional water is collected from what was an extremely damp tunnel. To the railway what was a nuisance is an asset to the water company.**

Chapter Six

FREIGHT AND

DEPARTMENTAL STOCK

F reight stock was the ultimate Cinderella, to most enthusiasts, and for the few who did photograph the nondescript wagon, 'black and white' was all but universal. When my father saw the IoW freight stock, he felt he had to cover a representative selection of it, in colour. The views which follow are possibly a unique colour record of some of this stock which should be of considerable value to the modeller. Unlike works views, they show timber bodied wagons as they appeared in service. One genuine IWR wagon is covered, the rest being Southern imports, mostly LB&SCR, but with LSWR goods brake vans included.

 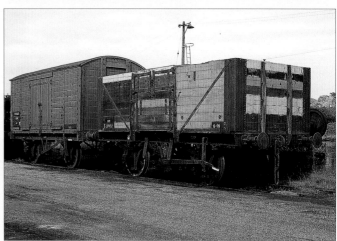

Top left: **S56046, recorded at Ryde on 29th October 1966, was one of three types of goods brake van in use on the island at the start of the 1960s. It was an L&SWR diagram 1541 'standard road van', of which half a dozen survived. They were provided with double doors in the sides to accommodate 'smalls', i.e. small quantities of goods for wayside stations. This made them ideal for permanent way duties as well, for tools could be easily stored there. They were 18ft over headstocks with a 10ft 6in wheelbase.**

Lower left: **DS46931, seen at Ryde St John's on 20th May 1964, was a former LB&SCR timber framed box van, one of three types sent to the island by the Southern in the 1920s and '30s. Less than a dozen survived by the early 'sixties, mostly as departmental stores vans.**

Top right: **S56058 at Ryde in October 1966. With balconies at each end and side duckets, it was an L&SWR diagram 1542 'large road van', and was 23ft 11in over headstocks with a 14ft wheelbase. Its principal use was on ballast trains. In the background is the ramp used to unload stock sent to the island for the forthcoming electrification. The second vehicle, S548, is another standard road van.**

Lower right: **The most modern freight stock in steam days were 88 of the diagram 1379 SR13T mineral wagons sent to the Island in 1948-49. They were built in the late 1920s, and replaced about 115 of the smaller and older Brighton opens. S27952, at St John's Road on 20th May 1964, typifies the latter-day condition of the wagon fleet. The Brighton van is DB46951.**

Top: **Perhaps the most celebrated of all the Island 'wagons' was 425S, which was built for the Isle of Wight Railway in 1865 by the Kirkstall Forge Company of Leeds. It was of 2 tons lift capacity, and was provided with a counter weight box which could be wheeled out along the tail to the appropriate distance. Instead of a conventional hook and 3-link coupling, it has a shackle and five short links, an arrangement common in the 1860s, but archaic long before 1900! This incredible vehicle stands in Ryde St John's works yard in April 1962. S28341, to the left of the crane, is an LB&SCR 5-plank drop door open wagon.**

Above left: **Our next illustration, taken at Ryde on 20th May 1964, covers no fewer than three wagons, plus the author, who inadvertently appeared at the back of the far**

wagon just as my father took this view. Given the historic significance of the wagons, I trust the reader will overlook this minor blemish! The nearest vehicle is DS60582, (tare weight 5.4) an LB&SCR diagram 1661 machinery truck, which was 16ft 6in over headstocks, with a 10ft 5in wheelbase. DS59043 and DS59044 (tare weight 4.13), are LB&SCR diagram 1616 single bolster wagons, 12ft over headstocks, with no more than a 7ft wheelbase. When the design appeared at the start of the 1880s, they were 'state of the art', but on the mainland most had vanished by the 1940s, and their survival on the island was another example of the time-warp in which the island's railways existed. No 59043 dated from 1907, and was sent to the Island in 1928. It was converted by BR as one of two adaptor wagons, with tube stock couplers at one

end, and survived at Sandown until 1991, when it was transferred to the steam railway.

Above right: **The most numerous class of wagons on the island were the diagram 1369 5-plank opens to a LB&SCR design, some of which were built by the SR soon after the Grouping. On the mainland, they would have been used for general merchandise rather than minerals, but they served both purposes on the Island. Most mainland examples had gone by the late 1940s, but about 150 were still in use on the island in the early 1960s. Although the line to Newport had been closed for eight months, when S19072 was photographed there on 29th October 1966, she is still under load, for periodic locomotive coal trips were still being worked from Medina Wharf through to Ryde.**

Between 1967 and 1992, a variety of departmental vehicles were transferred from the mainland, enabling the last of the steam age wagons, which had been retained for service use, to be discarded. In addition, Island Line became the last section of BR to retain an 03 shunter on its books. Through the courtesy of George Wheeler of Island Line, and with technical data from Roger Silsbury of the IoW Steam Railway, I have been able to illustrate a representative selection of departmental vehicles.

Top left: **The Southern atmosphere was still strong at Sandown in 1971, with an enamel and concrete 'running in' board, and green and cream paint still evident. The old Newport Junction bay at Sandown and stump of the branch served as the engineers depot. D2554 had been sent to the Island for departmental duties in 1966. She was a Hunslet 204 hp diesel mechanical 0-6-0, and dated from the dawn of the Modernisation Era on BR, for the class was introduced in 1955. She became successively 2554, 05 001 and eventually departmental loco 97 803. Predictably the last member of her class, No 2554 was withdrawn in April 1984, and later acquired by the Steam Railway. As with most of the smaller diesel shunters, she was powered by the well-proven Gardner 8L3 engine, but was restricted to a maximum of 15 mph, little more than half that which the more popular class 03s could do.**
R G Martindale

Centre left: **Two class 03 shunters were transferred to the Island for departmental duties. 03 079, built at Doncaster in 1960, was sent to the Island on 8th April 1984, and is seen at Sandown in 1987. Normally only used for nocturnal works and permanent way trains, her most celebrated use was during a Ryde Rail open day in 1986 when she provided brake van trips within the engineers sidings at Sandown. She has seen little use in recent years.**

Bottom left: **To assist with the 1980s modernisation, a second 03 shunter was transferred to the IoW on 30th June 1988. I am indebted to Andy Snell, Depot Manager at St John's Road for this view of 03 179 being unloaded by a pair of road cranes. The locomotive is in its original state, with full height cab. To the left is 1923 set 486 031. The 03s saw considerable use during the modernisation work, but thereafter were seldom put to work. 03 179 was officially withdrawn in October 1993, and 03 079 in June 1996, although the dates are notional, rather than significant, as both had been out of use for a substantial period. Their work has been taken over by a road rail tractor unit. At the time of going to press both locos remained on the Island, and will probably be included in the assets when the system is privatised.** Andy Snell

Top: **During the Autumn of 1988, 03 179 received a cut down cab, to enable it to operate through Esplanade tunnel. It was also at this time painted in full Network SouthEast livery. By August 1995, she lay out of use on the works head shunt at St John's Road, her NSE colours rather faded. It is doubtful if she will be used again. Owing to safety requirements, due to the third rail, public access is not ordinarily possible to this location, and this view and a number of others in this book, were only possible through the co-operation of management and staff of Island Line.**

Above left: **Two of the most fascinating wagons on Island Line are the adaptor wagons. When the first generation**

Underground cars came in the 1960s, a couple of old LB&SCR single bolster trucks had been modified as adaptor wagons, with tube stock couplings at one end, and conventional buffing gear at the other. By the 1980s they were in poor condition, and two of the four adaptor wagons used to move Waterloo & City stock between Waterloo and Stewarts Lane for repairs were sent to the Isle of Wight. ADB 453241 was built at Shildon in 1959 as a Lowfit, converted to an adaptor wagon in 1978, and transferred to the Island on 4th April 1992, and used immediately to move sets 009 and 010 from Sandown, where they had been off-loaded from road transporters, to Ryde. The Waterloo & City inscriptions and adaptor coupling are apparent in this August 1995 study.

Above: **Earlier in this book, I explained that eight of the 1938 sets were sent to the Island in 1989-90, and a further set, 009 in 1992. In the previous caption, I referred to a tenth set, 010. With the steady withdrawal of 1938 stock, it was felt that a spare pair of body shells would be useful for cannibalisation, in the event of any of the service cars being damaged at any time. Set 010 was not intended for operational purposes, but as a strategic reserve, and arrived on 8th April 1992, and is stored on the headshunt at Ryde St John's.**

Opposite page, top: **An interesting item recorded by photographer Klaus Marx in June 1967 has happily survived. The former Midland Railway crane, D429, which dated from the 1860s, had been acquired for the abortive Vectrail project, but passed to the Wight Locomotive Society in 1971, and is now at Haven Street. It had been sold to the IWCR in 1912, where it became Crane No 5, becoming 429S in Southern days.**

Opposite page, bottom: **Klaus felt that another crane he saw that day, IWR crane 425S, was too historic to be lost, and made a bid for this fascinating vehicle. In the event, the makers expressed interest, and the crane returned to its birthplace. In recording this June 1967 view, Klaus scored a unique double, for the lead vehicle in the 3-TIS and 4-VEC set in the background is S7S, which like 425S, has also been preserved, and in common with 425S, went off the Island, for it became a part of the London Transport historic collection upon withdrawal from IoW service!**

Above right: **By June 1994, DP101453, a 24 ton ballast hopper, TOPS code ZEO, was stored condemned at Sandown. It was the last ex-private owner wagon in the fleet, and had been built as an iron ore hopper by Metro-Cammell in 1940, and transferred to the island on 18th January 1978. It was typical of the iron ore hoppers ordered during the war to cope with the dramatic** increase in home iron ore quarrying. The original ORE lettering had started to show through later coats of paint.

Below: **DE263289, is an ex-LNER 25 ton Low-mac, code ZXV, built at Darlington in 1945. It was transferred to the Island on 17th August 1982, for use as a sleeper wagon, and was photographed at Sandown in June 1994.**

Bottom: **DW100715 is an 18 ton sleeper wagon, built in 1944 for the GWR, and transferred to the Island in July 1986. It is seen at Sandown in 1987. Officially condemned, it was still in occasional use in the early 'nineties.**

Top: **DB993598 is a 24 ton Dogfish Ballast hopper, new in 1960, making it the youngest wagon on the island in 1994. It arrived on 28th September 1989. With centre and side discharge capability, the three Dogfish have replaced the older and rarer Herring hoppers previously in use.**

Left: **DB460239, a 13 ton Medfit with drop sides, was built at Ashford in 1952 and transferred to the IoW in July 1986. It is used for general transport.**

Bottom left: **The last vehicle in this section is also the oldest. It is DS55724, a 1934 SR goods brake van, which came to the Island on 6th May 1967, so was also the longest serving departmental vehicle by 1994. Although the fascinating timber wagons of the 'sixties have gone, the choice is still astonishing with private owner, Southern, GWR, LNER and BR equipment!**

Above: **S55724, although at first sight a normal SR 'Pillbox' brake, is not the common 25 ton type, but one of the rarer 15 ton brakes, of which only 50 were built. Its Ashford plate has stood the ravages of 60 years remarkably well.**

Chapter Seven

THE CENTRAL

The Isle of Wight Central Railway was destined to become the largest of the Island railways, but unlike the Isle of Wight Railway, whose busy Ryde-Shanklin-Ventnor line ensured financial stability, the Central was always hard up. Had the Grouping not come when it did, in 1923, it is doubtful if the Central could have survived the advent of bus competition, and central and west Wight might have been denuded of railways before the mid-'thirties.

The oldest section of the Central, and indeed the earliest railway on the Island was the Cowes & Newport, authorised on 8th August 1859 and opened on 16th June 1862. An ominous portent for the future was that the opening of the line attracted little local excitement, and a contemporary report noted 'scarce half a dozen persons' travelled on the 8.15am, the first train out of Cowes on the opening day. The Isle of Wight Railway opened from Ryde to Shanklin in 1864, and obtained powers for a branch to Newport, but this was not built. Instead, a new company, the Ryde & Newport Railway was formed in 1872, to build a line from Smallbrook, 1½ miles south of St John's Road, to Newport. It opened on 20th December 1875. The C&N and R&N agreed to operate their lines under a joint committee.

In 1868, the Isle of Wight (Newport Junction) Railway was incorporated to build a 9½ mile line, which would strike south from Newport to Merstone, virtually at the centre of the island, and then east via Horringford and Alverstone to a junction with the IWR at Sandown. The Sandown to Horringford section was inspected by the Board of Trade in 1872 but opening was refused then and again in 1874 due to incomplete works. This section eventually opened on 1st February 1875, the same date as the section from Horringford to Shide. The next section, to Pan Lane, Newport, was inspected in August 1875, and rejected, but the problems were less severe this time, and the line opened on 6th October 1875. Even so, there was no physical connection with the C&N or R&N, and it was not until 1st June 1879 that the connecting viaduct, which joined the R&N viaduct just south of Newport station, was finished. The Newport Junction line was worked by the C&N/R&N Joint Committee,

but on 1st July 1887, the three concerns amalgamated to form the Isle of Wight Central Railway.

There was to be one further extension to the Central. This diverged off the Newport Junction line where it turned east at Merstone, and was to run via St Lawrence to Ventnor. Its history was even more eccentric than the rest of the Central. The first proposal was for a line from Shanklin on the IWR to the village of Chale, some six miles to the west. A new company, the Shanklin & Chale, was incorporated on 14th August 1885. In August 1889, it changed its starting and finishing points, its direction – it was now to run from north to south – and its name, to become the Newport, Godshill & St Lawrence Railway. The line opened from Merstone to St Lawrence, which is about a mile west of Ventnor, on 20th July 1897 and was extended to its own terminus in Ventnor on 1st June 1900. The 6¾ mile line was worked by the IWCR, and absorbed into that company on 8th April 1913. The IWCR, with 28½ route miles, and £651,166 expended on its lines by the close of 1915 was the largest of the Island companies, and with managers as forceful as C L Conacher, and later Russell Willmott, even managed to talk its way into the principal railways section of the prestigious Railway Year Book. Its neighbour, the more affluent IWR came under 'Remaining Railways owning Rolling Stock', but such coups notwithstanding, the Central was never as successful as the IWR. Its 400 shareholders were accustomed to not receiving a full preference dividend, let alone an ordinary dividend. Whilst all categories of IWR shareholders received a comparable holding of Southern shares in 1923, £100 of ordinary shares in the Central were computed as being worth just £3 cash.

There was also the line that 'got away' from the Central. This was the Freshwater, Yarmouth & Newport, which was authorised on 26th August 1880, opened to goods on 10th September 1888, and to passengers on 20th July 1889. It too was worked by the IWCR, but the FYN became restive, and decided to assume control of its own destinies, being advised by no less a person than Sir Sam Fay of the Great Central. Despite collapsing into receivership a few

weeks prior to 'independence', the FY&NR provided its own motive power and stock from 1st July 1913. Relations between the FYN and the Central were fraught for a time, and FYN passenger services ceased to use the Central station at Newport, stopping a short distance away on FYN property. The Southern did not value the FYN too highly, and if the IWCR shareholders had a poor deal, on the FYN, it was horrendous. Ordinary shares were simply cancelled, and even debenture holders did not get much !

The Merstone to Ventnor West line closed on 15th September 1952, the FYN on 21st September 1953, followed by the Newport to Sandown route on 6th February 1956. The line from Cowes to Smallbrook Junction closed on 21st February 1966, although coal workings between Medina Wharf and Ryde continued for some months.

This would have been the end of the story had it not been for the work of the Island's preservationists. The Wight Locomotive Society was formed to save one of the O2 tanks for static display, but fund raising was so successful that it was possible to acquire a number of bogie carriages as well. No 24 *Calbourne* was purchased for £900 on 22nd May 1967. A company called Sadler-Vectrail had plans to resurrect the Cowes to Ryde line as a rapid transit link, using modern tram technology, and apart from the stock acquired by the Wight Locomotive Society, some more was set aside for engineering purposes for Sadler-Vectrail. This project eventually fell through, and the WLS was able to acquire a number of items. Two other abortive preservation projects, one for the Westerham branch in Kent, and a plan to ship an IoW coach to Canada, also failed, enabling the WLS to acquire further vehicles.

As a result of the Sadler-Vectrail project, the Cowes line remained in situ for a considerable time, and *Calbourne* was not moved off BR property until 1969. As Smallbrook Junction had been severed during electrification work, it was not possible to move her by rail, so she was transported by road to Newport, where she lay until January 1971, when the WLS received a few days notice that they must vacate the site. *Calbourne* was steamed on 24th January 1971 to move the WLS stock by rail from Newport to Haven Street. A separate operating company, the Isle of Wight Railway Company Limited was formed in 1972 to run trains between Wootton and Haven Street, a distance of just under 2 miles. The two bodies were merged on 1st January 1990.

In the late 1980s, work began on an extension east from Haven Street to re-join the Shanklin line at Smallbrook. This opened on 20th July 1991. Apart from *Calbourne,* two Brighton 'Terriers' which had operated on the Island, but had been returned to the mainland in the 1940s, now run on the

steam railway. These, together with the mixture of bogie stock acquired when steam operations ended in the 1960s, and 4-wheelers rebuilt from vehicles which had once served as summer houses or chalets, give the line an 'authenticity' which is lacking on many preserved railways.

Photographs on the opposite page:

Top: **No 28 *Ashey*** waits time with an evening service from Ryde to Cowes on 20th May 1964. In a few minutes, she will be passing through the village she was named after. The leading coach S4158 is one of the five Brighton 7-compartment brake 2nds which survived into the 1960s. Unfortunately none of these interesting carriages were preserved.

Bottom: **As No 22 *Brading*** approaches St John's Road on 21st May 1964, the fireman is holding out the single line token for the section from Haven Street to Ryde for the signalman to collect, for winter working is still being followed and Smallbrook Junction has not yet opened for the summer season. Even if we did not see the staff handover, we could tell that winter working was in force, as all arms on the gantry to the left of the picture are in place. In summer, the two lower arms were removed.

This page, top right: **When the Ryde & Newport was first opened, it paralleled the single track Ventnor line of the IWR from Smallbrook to Ryde. To increase train capacity on what was a busy section of route, the Southern installed a small 20-lever signalbox at Smallbrook in May 1926. There was a scissors crossover just before the divergence, and the double track, from Ryde St John's Road to Smallbrook, provided much needed flexibility. As the winter service was less intensive than the summer workings, Smallbrook was only open from late May to September. In winter, it was taken out of use, the signal arms removed, and single track working reverted to from St John's Road, using the facing cross-over just beyond the platforms at St John's. No 24 *Calbourne* heads a Cowes train over the St John's cross-over on 20th May 1964, a few days prior to double track working commencing. Although not as smart as she had been the previous year, *Calbourne* was still a favoured engine, with the polished beading to the cab windows, gleaming whistle, and polished splasher beading. Alone out of the O2 tanks, No 24 has survived into preservation. Her name village was in West Wight, which was served by Calbourne & Shalfleet station, and was roughly the mid-point of the FYN.**

Centre right: **No 26 *Whitwell* passes Smallbrook Junction with the 4.28pm Cowes to Ryde Pier Head service on 7th August 1965. Klaus Marx**

Above left: **The fireman leans out from the cab as the signalman waits to receive the single line token at Smallbrook in August 1965.** Klaus Marx

Above right: **I just could not resist this enchanting portrait of *Freshwater* beside the signal cabin at Smallbrook in June 1994. As with the O2s, she carries a village name, this time the terminus of the Freshwater, Yarmouth & Newport line in West Wight. At the time of writing - August 1995, No 8 requires a new boiler costing £35,000. The IoW Steam Railway will welcome any donations towards this project.**

Left: No **8** *Freshwater* emerges from the tunnel-like portal of the bridge carrying the road from Ashey Down to Ryde, near Little Whitefield, in June 1994.

Below: **No 35 leaving Ashey on the 11.31am Cowes to Ryde Pier Head service on 17th September 1962.** K L Cook / Rail Archive Stephenson KLC 2478

Photographs on the opposite page:

Top: **I first visited Ashey Station on 20th August 1963, when Dad and I alighted from this Ryde to Cowes train. The engine crew of No 30 *Shorwell* gave us a few moments to scramble along the lineside to take this dramatic shot of the train pulling away en route to Cowes. The building in the background was the original station building, but had been taken out of use when Ashey was made an unmanned halt in the early 'fifties. Subsidence of the platform later prompted BR to provide a short new platform on the opposite side of the line, a few yards closer to Ryde.**

Bottom: **At almost the same spot over 30 years later, on 5th June 1994, we see No 8 *Freshwater* pull away from Ashey on another lovely summer day.**

Opposite page: **No 26 *Whitwell* was recorded, at what was to become the eventual western terminus of the Isle of Wight Steam Railway, Wootton Bridge, on 5th June 1961, with the 5.18pm Ryde Pier Head to Cowes train.**
K L Cook / Rail Archive Stephenson KLC 1588

Above: **No 24 *Calbourne* drifts into Haven Street, en route from Wootton to Smallbrook on 4th August 1995. During her 1993-94 overhaul, it was found that the 1930s enlarged bunker was badly worn, and in line with the IWSR policy of periodic changes, as evidenced with the 'Terriers' and their different liveries, it was decided to take the opportunity of running her with the original style bunker for some years. The line which drops away to the left is the headshunt for the Goosefield sidings, from which this view was taken. I am indebted to Len Pullinger, Chief Engineer of the IWSR for permission to film in a location not ordinarily open to the public.**

Below: **Whippingham station, which was built to serve Queen Victoria's retreat at Osborne House, over two miles to the north, but which was later made available to the public as well, was remote and isolated, and attracted little traffic. It was closed as an economy measure in September 1953.
No 24 *Calbourne* passes through the disused station on an LCGB special on 3rd October 1965.** Colour-Rail

Left: **Having run in a west-nor-west direction from Ashey to Whippingham, the line swung abruptly south so as to bridge the Medina at Newport. Civil engineering works on the last mile or so into Newport were heavy, with deep cuttings, a 73 yard long tunnel under the main road to Ryde, and the viaducts across the harbour itself. No 17 *Seaview* runs through the cutting short of the tunnel in August 1963.**

Above centre: **No 20 *Shanklin* clatters over the viaduct which carried the line across the Medina and Newport harbour just outside the station in August 1963. The motor vehicles are almost as fascinating as the train itself, for they include a Morris 8 ragtop, a Standard 9, an Austin 55, and a Wolseley 1500. As a youngster, I always found the approach to Newport, plunging into a tunnel, and then almost immediately onto a viaduct above the roof tops and harbour, one of the most thrilling of train trips.**
John Spencer Gilks / Colour-Rail BRS 762

Left: **Nowadays, the Newport by-pass bridges the river just a few feet down stream of where the railway bridge once stood. The warehouse on the left provides the only common reference point in these two scenes.**

Above: **The IoW (Newport Junction) Railway
to Sandown joined the Ryde & Cowes line
via a scissors cross-over just short of the
platforms at Newport. The two single tracks
ran side by side over the viaduct, before
diverging south of the station. A spotless
No 27 *Merstone*, which is signalled over the
scissors, and on to the Sandown line in May
1952, is the perfect introduction to the
Newport Junction line, which ran in a
southerly direction as far as Merstone, where
it turned east for Sandown.**
T B Owen / Colour-Rail BRS 602

Centre right: **At Merstone, the Newport,
Godshill & St Lawrence continued on south
to Ventnor West. S C Townroe photographed
No 32 *Bonchurch* running round the RCTS
special at Merstone Junction in May 1952.
The line to the left is to Sandown, and to the
right to Ventnor West. Pedestrian access to
the platforms was via the timbered
crossings, and along the path between the
railings in the foreground.**
S C Townroe / Colour-Rail BRS 828

Right: **No 35 *Freshwater* sweeps round the
curve off the Newport Junction line and into
Sandown station in October 1954. The
sidings to the right of the train once served a
brickworks, but have been used for stock
storage for many years, and are in
departmental use to this day, but still
referred to as the Brickfields siding.**
J McCann / Colour-Rail 975

Above: **When an RCTS special visited Ventnor West, S C Townroe photographed this tranquil backwater. No 32 *Bonchurch* occupies centre stage, but there is much else of interest, including the carmine-liveried SE&CR coaching stock, and the 13-lever signal cabin, which spent much of its life switched out when one-engine-in-steam working was in force between Merstone Junction and Ventnor.** S C Townroe / Colour-Rail BRS 400

Below: **W H G Boot visited Newport in May 1949, and took this classic study of Brighton E1 No 4 *Wroxall* in malachite green, but with Southern patch-painted out and British Railways added. The Island's railways had recovered from wartime neglect faster than most places, and by 1949-50 were particularly colourful, with some locomotives in SR colours, and others in BR lined black, and coaching stock in SR green or BR carmine. The shed and works at Newport were typical of many small depots throughout the country in the piecemeal accretion of structures.** W H G Boot / Colour-Rail BRS 115

Above: **One of our visits to Newport was on 21st August 1963. No 14 *Fishbourne* was waiting time with the 5.08pm Newport to Ryde.** In the introduction, I explained how my father would sometimes suggest that I take some slides to give me experience and confidence. I was apprehensive, as he would do it better, and I didn't want to mess up a view on a nice afternoon, but he insisted. This was the result. It was difficult to take, as I could only just get the engine in, but it worked. Fishbourne village is on the north coast, midway between Ryde and East Cowes. In the early 'sixties, guards and carriage cleaners complained about oil from the Westinghouse pumps splashing the end lookout windows on the brake coaches when the engines were running bunker first. To remedy this, a start was made on fitting engines with hinged metal shields which would catch the oil splashes. By the summer of 1963, Nos 14, 17, 18, 22 and 27 were so fitted. The pump shields, although solving the guards problem, were unpopular with the fitters, for the oil now dribbled down the inside of the shield and dropped on to the splasher and running plate, or sprayed back on to the pump, making it more unpleasant to work on. The shields were hinged, and if needs be, could be removed for maintenance purposes. This occurred regularly, and re-fitting the shields afterwards was sometimes overlooked. I understood from one of the fitters involved that this was sheer forgetfulness, and never deliberate, but be that as it may, the pump shields soon vanished. Having seen a locomotive with the pump shield open, and how foul it looked, caked in oil and muck, I could not have blamed the fitters had their forgetfulness been intentional!

Below: **Although Ryde was by far the busier station, Newport had been the Island's** crossroads with the FYN and Sandown lines connecting into the Cowes-Ryde route. In many ways, Newport was the more imposing station, with its viaduct approach from the south, long platforms, and mass of sidings to the north. We are looking north towards Cowes from the down platform in April 1962. The locomotive shed, disused for loco-motive purposes from 1958, still stands in the background behind the up platform canopy.

Top left: **The FYN approach to Newport was almost as dramatic as the Ryde line, for the railway was carried on two long viaducts, one of arched construction, the other of wrought iron girders on spidery columns. The seldom photographed No 34 *Newport*, clatters on to Hunnyhill viaduct in April 1953.** Colour-Rail

Top right: **Colour views on the FYN are understandably hard to find, as the line closed on 21st September 1953. Equally difficult to find have been colour photographs of No 34 *Newport*, which arrived on the island in May 1947 and was withdrawn in August 1955. Apart from having the shortest career of any of the Adams O2 tanks on the island, No 34 was one of the first to be disposed of. This portrait of No 34, near Carisbrooke in June 1953, with a Freshwater train, is especially welcome.** S C Townroe / Colour-Rail BRS 830

Above: **This magnificent portrait of No 32 *Bonchurch* in SR malachite green, but patch painted and re-lettered 'British Railways', was taken on an RCTS special in May 1952. It shows the rural surroundings of Freshwater station.** T B Owen / Colour-Rail BRS 604

Left: **No 36 *Carisbrooke*, in unlined BR black, is at the platform at Freshwater in April 1953. Facilities comprised a run-round loop and three sidings.** Colour-Rail

Below: **Yarmouth has always been the customary starting point for visits to one of the Island's most celebrated attractions, Alum Bay, with its astonishing multi-coloured cliffs, and the Needles. The most exciting way to get there is via Southern Vectis route 42 with its open top double deckers. Bristol LD6G No 500 was new to the company in 1956, was sold out of service in the 1970s and re-acquired in 1993 to augment the open top fleet. No 500 has just left the bus terminal which adjoins the slipway for the ferry service from Lymington.**

Centre left: **No contemporary colour views appear to exist of Yarmouth station, but the buildings survive little altered from railway days, save for the loss of a short platform canopy. They are used as a Youth Centre, and it is good to see them put to a positive use.**

Left: **Conventional wisdom proclaims that 13 to 15 years is a normal 'lifespan' for a bus. If so, CDL899, Southern Vectis No 502, was starting her fifth life when she was photographed roaring up the formidable climb from Alum Bay to Headon Warren on 8th August 1995. CDL899 was new to the company on 19th July 1939, and commenced life as a Bristol K5G 'highbridge' or normal height double decker with an Eastern Coach Works 56-seat body. Conversion to open top came in 1959, and she continues to tackle the formidable climb out of Alum Bay each summer. She is probably the oldest bus to have remained in continuous passenger service with her original operator anywhere in the world.**

Top: **No 32 *Bonchurch* departs from Newport on the 5.18pm Ryde Pier Head to Cowes service on 9th June 1961.** K L Cook / Rail Archive Stephenson KLC 1713

Left: **Freight and shunting engines received much less attention from photographers than passenger types, and it is astonishing that the earliest colour view known to the author of the IoW railways is this study of a former LB&SCR E1 tank, No 2 *Yarmouth*, shunting at Newport in the late 1930s. The E1s saw a great deal of use on freight services, including the regular coal trains from Medina Wharf to Ryde. The tank, splasher and footplate lining in the Maunsell style are all visible. Other items of interest are the olive green coaching stock, platform barrow and 5-plank ex-Brighton open wagon.** Colour-Rail

Left: **Newport had been signalled by two cabins, the larger at the north end of the station which controlled the yard connections and the FYN junction, survived to the end of steam services in 1966. We are looking from the up running line with the FYN branch siding in the background.**

Above: **The way in which facts and figures were manipulated in the mid-'sixties to guarantee the closure of the Island's railways still rankles, and remains a topic of conversation amongst Islanders to this day. Despite such Machiavellian antics, the Ministry of Transport found that the Ryde to Shanklin section should not be closed, due to the intolerable pressure it would place on the roads on summer Saturdays, but there was no reprieve for the Shanklin to Ventnor, or Ryde-Newport-Cowes lines. Cowes services terminated on 21st February 1966. It is 29th October, and eight months have passed since services to Newport ended, but other than for the rust on the rails, and a certain amount of vegetation, one might almost expect to see a train appear from Cowes at any moment. A string of wagons occupy the stump of the FYN line which closed in the early fifties, but which was used for stock storage until Newport itself closed. To the right, coaching stock surplus to the steam operation between Ryde and Shanklin awaits its fate. Today, the Newport by-pass sweeps across the site, and it is hard to imagine that this impressive array of tracks ever existed.**

Above: **In tracing the Southern Vectis story, I have decided to bring in this 1971 view of NDL768G, a short 35-seater Bristol LH, at this point, for the LH was the successor in the 35-43 seat range to the discontinued SU.**

No 832 was a 1969 delivery but unlike many vehicles which served for 20 years or more, this one had gone in half that time. 465 ADL, on the far left, was the last SU to join the fleet. R G Martindale

Bottom right: **With the trains gone, provision of public transport for Newport was left to the buses. In 1971 Southern Vectis No 846, 459ADL, a Bristol SU of 1963 prepares to pull out of Newport bus station en route to Whitepit Lane on the then 15A route, serving the south side of the town and Carisbrooke. The 30-36 seat SU was a rare machine with just 181 examples built between 1960 and 1966 for Bristol group operators.**
R G Martindale

Above: **No 35 *Freshwater* heads the 4.15pm Ryde Pier Head to Cowes service, near Medina Wharf, on a lovely 8th June 1961.**
K L Cook / Rail Archive Stephenson KLC 1639

Below: **Some locomotives in a particular class always seem to be rather camera shy. As far as the colour record is concerned, relatively few shots of No 25 *Godshill* have turned up. Here, a very clean No 25, is seen**

shunting at Medina Wharf, on 9th June 1961.
K L Cook / Rail Archive Stephenson KLC 1695

Opposite page, top: **Mill Hill station, lying just south of the sharply curved Mill Hill tunnel, served the southern outskirts of Cowes. No 22 *Brading* enters the station with a Newport train in August 1965.**
J P Mullett / Colour-Rail BRS 563

Opposite page, bottom: **No 3 *Ryde* is depicted at the head of the 1952 RCTS special at Cowes. The locomotive is in unlined black, with 'British Railways' lettering, whilst the carriages are in the all-over carmine livery adopted by BR for non-corridor stock. It seems strange to see red coaches in the IoW, for we are so conditioned by Southern green, and the early return to green on the Southern Region.** T B Owen / Colour-Rail BRS 594

Above: **No 25 *Godshill*** pulls away from Cowes in 1960. This engine was withdrawn in December 1962, and when I was working on the book, presented serious problems. I had photographed her in black and white at Cowes shortly before withdrawal, but the slides we had were not quite up to the standard required for reproduction in this book. Then shortly before the book went to press two good images of No 25 appeared, that reproduced on page 78 and the picture presented here. The only engines to operate in BR service on the island which we have not been able to find colour photographs of are E1 tank No 1, O2 tank No 23 *Totland*, which was the first of the

Adams tanks to go, in August 1955, and the solitary Brighton E4, 2510, which was tried out on the Island between February 1947 and April 1949. Colour-Rail

Below: **No 30 *Shorwell*** simmers in the platform at Cowes on 22nd August 1963, as passengers hurry by. When the train is empty, she will propel the coaches back down the platform, set forward, and run round via the escape cross-over which is located some distance down the platform. After running round, the train will be propelled back so as to be convenient for passengers boarding it.

Above: **No 28** *Ashey* **has backed her train into the platform, to the usual departure position, in this fascinating winter time scene in January 1963. Unusually for the Island, there is a coating of snow on the platforms. The passenger stock is exceptionally grimy in this winter scene.**
L Folkard / Colour-Rail BRS 675

Centre right: **By way of contrast to the other pictures of Cowes on this and the preceding pages, is this view taken on 11th September 1968. More than two and a half years have elapsed since passenger services ceased, but as we look from platform 1 towards the signalbox, the station is still intact.** R J Barry

Bottom right: **Cowes station fronted on to Carvel Lane, and was flanked to the north by Terminus Road. We look from Terminus Road in August 1995 to the modern bus station, where Leyland Olympian 716 picks up passengers. Carvel Lane, to the left, is much wider than in railway days, and the station buildings were located where the bus pull-off point is. To the right of the view is a modern supermarket. I selected a working showing the No 2 route, as this runs via Smithards Lane (once a level crossing on the Newport line), Newport, Blackwater, and Godshill, to Sandown, all locations one could have reached by train until the 1950s!**

C. 44351. COWES, I.O.W. FLOATING BRIDGE.

Left: **A chain ferry, or floating bridge connects East and West Cowes, and I have selected two illustrations. The first is from a pre-1914 colour postcard showing the bridge as it was more than eighty years ago.**

Centre left: **Our second illustration of the floating bridge was taken in August 1995. As with so much on the Island, the change is less apparent than one might have expected over an 80 year period, and other than for the motor vehicles and plunging necklines and short skirts of some of the lady passengers, the visitor of 1910 would feel at home in the 1990s.**

Left: **The Red Funnel car ferry terminal is within a few yards of the chain ferry slip in East Cowes. The *Netley Castle* which entered service in 1972 after various teething troubles, and which was the first double ended ferry in the Red Funnel fleet, is framed by the link span at East Cowes. The *Netley Castle* was fitted with four rotatable propeller units for propulsion and steering, and was designed never to need turning, one end being the 'Southampton' end and the other the 'Cowes' end. Concepts such as bows and stern vanished. I have selected this end-on view rather than a three quarters angle partly because of the dramatic composition, but more importantly because it shows how additional car space was provided in 1980 by widening out the hull on the western side into a sponson, giving the vessel a curious asymmetrical appearance from end-on.**

Chapter Eight

RYDE WORKS

Over the years, I have visited many railway stations, and I cannot think of one which was better laid out for the enthusiast than St John's Road. With an overbridge which offered photographic opportunities at the north end, a signal box just off the south end of the platforms, and attractive buildings on both platforms, the photographer 'had it made'. Add to that a steam shed next to the up platform, and what more could one ask for ? Being the Isle of Wight, you got more, with a works adjoining the down platform, so that you could see whatever was happening in the works yard. When you add a friendly and obliging staff, it gets even better.

The O2s have gone, as has the steam shed, and the works now serves as maintenance and running depot, but a visit to the works in 1994 showed that the friendliness was as great as we had first experienced some 30 years earlier when I had made my first visit there to photograph behind the scenes in Ryde works.

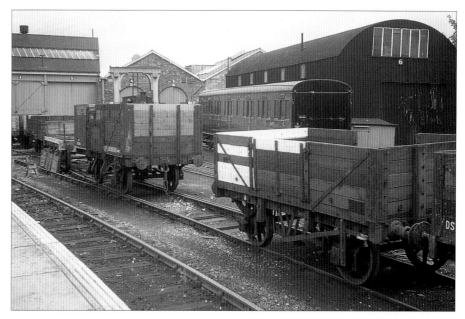

Right: **Traditional freight working and timber-bodied wagons were disappearing by the early 'sixties, but in this portrait of the works yard on 21st August 1963, wagon stock is well to the fore. The nearest vehicle is a 5-plank LB&SCR diagram 1369 open, which has received several replacement planks at the far end. The next vehicle is one of the 88 diagram 1379 steel framed mineral wagons shipped to the Island in 1948-49. Beyond that is one of the 4-plank dropside ballast wagons, of which several varieties existed, some imported by the Southern, others rebuilds from IWR/IWCR parts and imported bodywork. This wagon has received a new headstock, a new side rail, and much new body planking. It is astonishing to see so comprehensive a rebuild of a pre-grouping timber-bodied wagon at so late a date. The works buildings comprise the carriage shop, roads 1 to 3, which included the carpenters shop, the machine shop, roads 4 and 5, and the wagon shop, the black corrugated iron building, road 6, with the smithy behind it. The two-road brick building in the centre of the picture, (roads 4 and 5) was the original IWR loco shed, which was replaced in 1874 by a corrugated iron edifice on the opposite side of the line.**

Lower right: **A Drummond boiler, removed from No 18 *Ningwood* a few weeks earlier, sits on departmental flat DS439 by the sheerlegs in April 1962. We can study not only the dome mounted safety valves, which were usually hidden by the dome cover, but the telescopic nature of the boiler barrel. The boiler truck had commenced life as IWR carriage truck No 76, and was transferred to departmental use by the SR. It was used to convey boilers between Ryde works and St. Helen's Quay where they were craned on to a barge for transfer to Eastleigh. Latterly it was confined to works duties only.**

Above: **The Ryde depot of the 1990s, although using many of the old buildings, has been totally transformed. Set 008 sits on the elevated inspection/maintenance track at Ryde Train Care Depot, as it is now called. The 'Think Quality' slogan is amusing, but true, it reads –** *'When we do it right no-one remembers. When we do it wrong no-one forgets'*.

Centre left: **Car S20, sits outside the works in 1987. The old road numbers above 1,2,3 and 5 roads are still in evidence, albeit that 5 has slipped to a rather strange angle. This view makes an interesting comparison with the first illustration in this section where timber bodied wagons occupy much of the foreground.**

Left: **With the imminent arrival of the 1938 class 483 stock, the works received a facelift in 1988, with elevated roads to permit easy access to the underfloor traction motors on the new cars. Sets 003 and 007 bring the story up to 1994. In another 30-35 years, roughly the period covered by these illustrations of Ryde works, there will be more changes. I am sure they will be just as fascinating.**

Chapter Nine

DESPAIR AND REBIRTH

Above left: **At first sight this is a confusing view, for what is No 27 *Merstone* doing at the country end of a train in the up platform at St John's Road? If we look down the train we will see a second engine. Although *Merstone* is not in good condition, it seems improbable that two engines are needed for three carriages. If I say that this view was taken in October 1966, Wight devotees will know the answer. Owing to electrification works at Pier Head, services were terminated at Esplanade from September 1966. As run round facilities did not exist at Esplanade, all trains had to be banked from St John's Road, the banker on the up journey becoming the train engine on the next down run, and vice versa. On the down run, the rear engine would be detached at St John's and go to shed for servicing, ready to bank the next working to Esplanade.**

Above right: **A late afternoon sun gleams on No 24 *Calbourne* as she**

runs round her train at Shanklin on 29th October 1966. The evening sun seemed somehow fitting at the time, and alone out of the O2 tanks, the sun *was* to shine on Calbourne. The attempt to save her was to mushroom into the wonderful Isle of Wight Steam Railway which we can all enjoy today.

Below: **It is 29th October 1966, and steam had just two months to run, as the Drummond-boilered No 31 *Chale* approaches Sandown. Although still lined out and with her tanks commendably clean, her smokebox shows considerable corrosion and evidence of over-heating at some time. Dad and I both felt sad that the engines we had come to know were nearing the end of their lives. Along with No 24, she was retained for engineering duties after steam services ended in December 1966, but sadly went to the breakers afterwards, a last minute preservation bid having proved abortive.**

Top left: **By 1966, the writing was on the wall for the O2 tanks. Steam workings between Ryde and Shanklin were to cease at the end of the year, and electric services would begin the following Spring. It was a bleak prospect for whilst the Bluebell Railway indicated that standard gauge preservation was feasible, various schemes in other parts of the country had collapsed. Klaus Marx visited Ryde in August 1966, and found a massive pile of scrap on the old coal road at St John's Road shed. One of the breaker's men was applying the torch as he was there. The locomotive in the foreground is No 26 *Whitwell*. No 14 *Fishbourne*, over by the shed, still has a few months to live.** Klaus Marx

Top right: **This sad line up of engines was recorded at Newport on the 16th June 1967. It comprises Nos 22 *Brading*, 14 *Fishbourne*, 33 *Bembridge* and 17 *Seaview*.** Klaus Marx

Above: **On the same day, this was all that remained of No 28 *Ashey*. Interestingly this slide had to wait until 1995 for a positive identification of the engine, but with the aid of other views taken by Klaus which eliminated several engines, and by using a microscope, I was able to deduce that it had to be in the 20s, and the second numeral had a rounded top! 28 became the only possible candidate.** Klaus Marx

Right: **By contrast with the sad pictures on the page opposite, the end of the steam era on the Isle of Wight coincided with the first flowerings of what was to become the Isle of Wight Steam Railway. The only surviving O2, No 24 *Calbourne* had 'gone green', by 1971, and a start had been made with lining out. At this date, she was facing towards Ryde, something which had not been seen on the Island since the closure of the Newport Junction line in the 'fifties. This had taken place when she was moved by road from Ryde to Newport in 1969. She was later turned to face Newport.** R G Martindale

Centre right: **Moving to the other end of the station, the Wight Locomotive Society had only just acquired the 2 mile stretch between Haven Street and Wootton. In 1971 the comprehensive sheds and workshops of the 1990s did not exist, and except for the crane sitting on the running line, it would be easy to believe that one was still in BR days, with a train heading for Ryde in the platform. The grassy platform is not a result of closure, but because so few people used this end of the station, which was remote from the exit, the grass was not worn away. One applauds the wonderful achievements of the preservationists, but at the same time, it is nice to have the grass era on record.** R G Martindale.

Bottom right: **D2059, a class 03 shunter, came to the Island in November 1988, and is seen six years later at Haven Street. Built in 1959, the locomotive last worked for BR at Colchester Depot from where it was withdrawn from service in July 1987. Its final BR number was 03 059. The locomotive was fitted with dual vacuum and air brakes, the latter being compatible with the traditional Westinghouse brake, used on the Island. The 03 is useful for shunting and as a standby in case of the failure of one of the steam engines.**

Above left: **In restoring the signalling at Haven Street, the Steam Railway have done a magnificent job, and have kept the character of this fascinating cabin which is in the front room of the station building. Note the inscription on the 'push-pull' lever No 5. A push-pull lever has nothing to do with a push-pull or motor train, but is a method of using one lever for two purposes. Its 'normal' position is not back in the frame, but in the mid point, and when pushed works one connection, and when pulled a different connection. Where a frame cannot be extended, it provides an answer to a shortage of levers.**

Above right: **At Smallbrook Junction the facing points are worked from a small 2-lever frame at the west end of the loop. This uses a traditional Stevens & Sons knee frame of the type to be found on the Island in steam days. Looking at this photograph, it is hard to imagine that this has been created by the preservationists, and not a miraculous survival from long ago.**

Bottom left: **In the 1930s, the SR instituted a 'Best Kept Station' competition, the winner holding a commemorative seat for the year. In the early days it was usually Newport or Shanklin, but from the late 'fifties Haven Street had a run of victories. I had heard of 'The Seat' but first encountered it at Haven Street, and it is appropriate that it should now be in the museum there.**

Above: **An impressive collection of artifacts has been gathered in the museum at Haven Street, including the nameplates from two of the Beyer Peacock 2-4-0Ts built for the Isle of Wight Railway, *Shanklin* dated from 1864, and *Ventnor* from 1868. They were withdrawn in 1927 and 1925 respectively.**

Above: **My first encounter with SR cattle wagon 46924 was in the 1960s, when it was in departmental use. Sadly it was in an awkward position for photography and thus had to go unrecorded at that time. As the last surviving ex-LB&SCR cattle wagon, it was shipped back to the mainland in 1967 for inclusion in the National Collection. By arrangement with the National Railway Museum, it has returned to the Island, where it has been restored to Southern Railway livery. Six of these vehicles were shipped to the Island in 1927-29, but with a falling off in livestock traffic, three were converted to closed vans in 1935.**

Top: **Apart from *Calbourne*, and two Brighton 'Terriers', the Steam Railway sometimes operates *Invincible*, a Hawthorne Leslie 0-4-0ST built in 1915 for Woolwich Arsenal. She later saw service at the Royal Aircraft Establishment, Farnborough, before being sold for scrap, rescued, and moved to the Isle of Wight in 1971. From 1973 until 1976, she was the only workable steam engine on the line.**

Above: **No 198 *Royal Engineer* is a Hunslet-designed 'Austerity' 0-6-0ST, also known by enthusiasts by its L&NER classification of J94. No 198 was built for the MoD in 1953, and saw service at Steventon, Bicester and Long Marston. In 1991 it was acquired by the Royal Corps of Transport Museum Trust, but as this project will not open for some time, was placed on loan to the IWSR from 1992. The Westinghouse fittings are to enable No 198 to haul passenger trains, though a handful of 'Austerities' did carry such equipment in War Department service.**

Above: **Two of the LB&SCR's famous A1X 'Terrier' 0-6-0Ts have returned to the Island where they once worked. Built in 1878 as LB&SCR No 40 *Brighton*, this engine was sold to the Isle of Wight Central Railway in 1902. Numbered 11 and given the name *Newport* by the SR in 1930, it returned to the mainland in 1947. Withdrawn as BR No 32640, in September 1963, it was then bought by Butlin's for display at their holiday camp in Pwllheli. Acquired for use on the Island, it arrived back in 1973. Extensive restoration work took a further 16 years. Restored as IWC No 11, the locomotive is seen here leaving Haven Street for Wootton on 20th April 1992.** Chris Milner

Below: **The IWSR's other 'Terrier' was built for the LB&SCR and sold to the L&SWR for use on the Lyme Regis branch. It was hired for use by the Freshwater, Yarmouth & Newport Railway, arriving in 1913 in L&SWR livery. Later purchased, the locomotive was subsequently named *Freshwater* and remained on the Island until 1949. Back on the mainland, it saw service at Newhaven and on the Hayling Island branch. Sold in 1963, it had a spell as a static exhibit outside a public house. It was then donated to the IWSR in 1979 and entered service in 1981. It received FYN livery in 1989; and is recorded at Haven Street on 15th August of that year.** Mike Everton

Above: **The signalman is ready to exchange single line tokens as No 8 drifts into Haven Street in 1994. The remarkably authentic Southern Railway atmosphere recreated on the IWSR is evident from this picture.**

Below: **In 1994 IWC No 11 was repainted into BR early 1950s livery as No 32640. In this guise it is about to leave Haven Street station on a photographer's special on 21st May 1994. This view recalls memories of its service on the branch from Havant to Hayling Island in the 1960s. In the siding to** the right can be glimpsed the Railway's 1953 (or 1954) vintage Wickham permanent way trolley No DS 3320 (ex B5W and PWM3766). Powered by a Ford side-valve petrol engine and equipped with chain drive, this vehicle came to the IWSR after service with BR on the Island. Chris Milner

Top left: **The original station at Wootton was on the west side of the road between Wootton Bridge and Staplers. Somewhat improbably, the station buildings were actually located within one of the arches of the road bridge itself ! It was in a clay cutting, and subject to regular earth movements, which led to its premature closure in the 1950s. The preservation era station is on the east side of the road, and was opened in 1986. When one looks at the Southern character, one's initial impression is of an excellent refurbishment of an 'old' station. The authenticity of what is a new station masks the full merit of what has been achieved by the preservationists. This view of No 11, about to run round its train, was taken on 20th April 1992. Chris Milner**

Centre: **A vintage bus service is now operated by a Bedford devotee, John Woodhams, from Wootton station to East Cowes, Osborne House and Barton Manor. The pride of the Woodhams fleet is JT8077, a 1937 Bedford WTB with a 25 seat Duple body. It was acquired by John in 1992, and is seen in Victoria Grove in East Cowes on 6th August 1995.**

Bottom: **The more normal guise of the former FYN No.2 is as SR No 8 *Freshwater*. The locomotive approaches the BR-built platform and shelter at Ashey with a Smallbrook train on 5th June 1995. Once again, the character created by the Steam Railway is impeccable.**

Right: **The Ryde-Shanklin line provides a valuable all-year transport service, and reduces congestion on the busy east coast roads. The 1938 tube stock continues the Isle of Wight's great tradition of making use of second hand equipment from the mainland. Obligingly the crew have hung on for a few seconds in case any passengers are cutting it fine to catch the last train of the day, the 22.12 from Shanklin on the night of the carnival in August 1995. In a few moments, the crew will lock up the station, and quiet will descend until the following morning. They will make up the lost time en route, for the 1938 stock has good acceleration. As with the 1923 cars, the maximum speed is 45 mph, but improved motor and body design permitted a reduction from 178 kW motors to 130 kW motors, whilst retaining the same performance. They are a few inches longer and wider than the older stock.**

Left: **Eight sets of the 1938 stock were delivered to the Island in 1989-90. However it became clear that an additional set was required, and the latest stock to enter service on the Island at the time of writing, is Set 009, which was shipped to the IoW on 9th April 1992. It forms the second part of a 4-car train which snakes over the cross-over at Esplanade station on 4th August 1995.**

Below: **Sets 002/006 were recorded from the now disused down platform at Esplanade on their way to Pier Head on 7th August 1995.**

Top: **In the opening pages of this book, we portrayed some of the ferries which have operated over the last 50 years. It seems appropriate, near the end of the book, to look at some of their modern counterparts. The modern ferries do not have the same grace as their predecessors, but in the motor age, do a job the older vessels could not have tackled. The first step towards the modern car ferry was taken by the Southern Railway in 1927, when they introduced a new vehicular ferry service between Portsmouth and Fishbourne, a small village on Wootton Creek. Two double-ended ferries with bow and stern ramps were built in 1927-28, and at the time were revolutionary. Along with a third vessel, built in 1930, they served until 1961, when they were replaced by much larger vehicle ferries. Rising demand has led to vessels such as the *St Helen*, operated by Wightlink – the name adopted after Sealink services were privatised in the**

1980s – and sold to the Bermuda-based Sea Containers Group. Unlike most of the Sealink routes which were later sold to Stena, Sea Containers retained the IoW services until 1995. Four Voith-Schneider fitted vessels, built between 1983 and 1990, serve the route today. All accommodate 1,000 passengers and 142 cars, and although tonnage varies, the 1983-built *St Helen* of 2,983grt being the largest, length and other dimensions are identical. Although *St Helen* is a far cry from the 1928 rampboats, the principle is the same, and the sylvan setting, with trees almost to the water's edge on both banks of the creek, is scarcely altered from the day the SR commenced the service.

Above left: **The arrival of the 'Saints' on the Fishbourne route displaced the existing 1970s 'C' class ships from Fishbourne to Yarmouth. There were four ships in total, the original *Cuthred* of 1971, which was**

somewhat underpowered, and the three sister ships, *Caedmon*, *Cenwulf* and *Cenred*, built by Robb, Caledon Shipbuilders Ltd of Dundee in 1973. Car capacity was boosted in 1977-78 by installation of hydraulically operated mezzanine liftable car decks. *Cuthred* was withdrawn in 1987, but the remaining three ships were still used on the Yarmouth route in 1995. *Cenwulf* is at the berth, as a second vessel rounds the pier and heads for Lymington.

Above right: **Apart from the use of the then revolutionary Voith-Schneider drive as long ago as 1938, the IoW has seen other hi-tech services, including hovercraft, hydrofoils and 'cats'. *Shearwater V* is a 32-knot hydrofoil accommodating 67 passengers and was built for Red Funnel by Cantiere Navale Rodriguez at Messina in 1980. These fast craft take just 22 minutes between Southampton and the fast craft terminal at West Cowes.**

Above: **Pride of the Red Funnel fleet in the 1990s are the massive *Red Falcon*, *Red Osprey*, and *Red Eagle*. Their names mark a departure from the Castle theme adopted early in the car ferry era, with vessels such as *Norris Castle*, *Carisbrooke Castle* or *Osbourne Castle*. Built by Ferguson Ship-builders, Port Glasgow, and launched in** April 1994, *Red Osprey*, seen above, is **82.4m in length, carries 140 cars and 895 passengers, and is driven by the Voith Schneider system which has been associated with the Island for so long. She is seen in a dramatic aerial shot en route to East Cowes early in 1995. At 2,881 tonnes, the Raptor class ferries offer a vast increase in carrying** capacity compared to the early car ferries. **The third ship in the class, *Red Eagle*, has additional covered accommodation, and is 3,068grt. After trial runs on 17th April 1996, a formal reception took place the following day, and she entered daily service on 19th April.** Photograph courtesy of Red Funnel Ferries

Above: **We close with these two recent views of the Island's railways. On 19th April 1992 electric unit No 003 arrives at St John's Road on a service from Shanklin to Ryde Pier Head. The two generations of ex-London Transport tube stock have become as closely linked in our memories, and as much a part of the Island's distinctive railway history, as the steam locomotives which they replaced.** Chris Milner

Below: **The Island's railways today, still differ from the mainland and are still full of charm and interest for the many visitors who flock to this distinctive and picturesque island. No 24 *Calbourne*, in her first full summer in traffic after rebuilding, enters Wootton station on Friday 4th August 1995 with an afternoon service on the delightful Isle of Wight Steam Railway.**